Carola-
platz
Carolabrücke
Albertbrücke
Terrassenufer
...enufer
Grunaer Straße
Güntzstraße
Stübelallee
Lennéstraße
Hauptallee
Fürstenallee
22
23
24
AF397369

DRESDEN IN DREI ZEITEN — **David Blum** — DRESDEN IN THREE ERAS

DRESDEN IN DREI ZEITEN — **David Blum** — DRESDEN IN THREE ERAS

David Blum

DRESDEN IN DREI ZEITEN
DRESDEN IN THREE ERAS

Damals —— Then

Zerstört im Zweiten Weltkrieg —— Destroyed during World War II

Heute —— Nowadays

E. A. Seemann

INHALT — TABLE OF CONTENTS

VORWORT — INTRODUCTION

DAS ALTE DRESDEN

Blühe, deutsches Florenz, mit Deinen Schätzen
der Kunstwelt!
Stille gesichert sei Dresden-Olympia uns!

Johann Gottfried Herder[1]

Wenn einem Kunsthistoriker eine Hauptverkehrsstraße gewidmet, wenn ein öffentlicher Platz nach ihm benannt und ein Denkmal für ihn errichtet wird, dann muss es sich um einen besonderen Vertreter seiner Art handeln. Fritz Löffler hat bei den Staatlichen Kunstsammlungen Dresden sowie beim Landesamt für Denkmalpflege Sachsen seine Spuren hinterlassen. Er hat über Otto Dix, Hans Theo Richter und viele weitere Künstler publiziert. Vor allem aber hat er das Kunststück vollbracht, eine Epoche seiner Stadt vor dem Vergessen zu bewahren. Dafür wurde er in einer Umfrage der *Dresdner Neuesten Nachrichten* zu einem der „100 Dresdner des 20. Jahrhunderts"[2] gewählt. ——— Löffler gilt als einer der wichtigsten Chronisten Dresdens. Sein Hauptwerk legte er nach dem Zweiten Weltkrieg vor, ein Buch, das die Stadt, die von den Bomben der Alliierten zerstört worden war, wieder erfahrbar machen sollte. „Du hast jetzt die Chance", umriss Löffler einmal in einem Interview seine Motivation, „nochmal zusammenzufassen, was diese Stadt geistig und künstlerisch war, zumindest auf dem Sektor der Stadtbaukunst. Das alles muß

OLD DRESDEN

Flourish, German Florence, with your treasures
of art!
May our Dresden Olympia be always protected!

Johann Gottfried Herder[1]

When a main thoroughfare has been dedicated to an art historian, when a public square bears his name and a monument has been erected in his honour, he must be an extraordinary representative of his field. Fritz Löffler left his mark on the Dresden State Art Collections as well as on the Saxony State Office for Historical Preservation. He published works on Otto Dix, Hans Theo Richter, and many other artists, but, above all, he managed to save an entire era of his city from falling into oblivion, a feat for which he was voted one of 'Dresden's 100 leading figures of the twentieth century' in a survey conducted by the regional newspaper *Dresdner Neueste Nachrichten*.[2] ——— Löffler is considered one of Dresden's most important historians. After the Second World War, he published his magnum opus, a book intended to recreate the city that had been destroyed by Allied bombs. In an interview, Löffler once described his motivation for this work as follows: 'Now is your chance to summarise what defined the city intellectually and artistically, at least in terms of its architecture. It all needs to be seen again. Dresden must be seen again. I wanted to preserve the myth of Dresden.'[3] In 1955, the first edition of *Das alte Dresden* (Old Dresden) was published by Sachsenverlag; it would not be the last. ——— Beginning in 1966, Löffler's book was published by E. A. Seemann; it has appeared in seventeen editions so far. In the foreword, the former Conservator for the State of Saxony Gerhard Glaser notes, 'Originally

noch einmal erscheinen. Dresden muß noch einmal da sein. Ich wollte den Mythos Dresdens bewahren."[3] 1955 brachte der Sachsenverlag *Das alte Dresden* in einer ersten Ausgabe heraus – es sollte nicht die letzte bleiben. —— Ab 1966 erschien der Löffler bei E. A. Seemann, mittlerweile kommt er auf 17 Auflagen. „Ursprünglich als postume Würdigung der 1945 untergegangen Stadt gedacht", schreibt der damalige Sächsische Landeskonservator, Gerhard Glaser, im Vorwort, „wurde das Buch zum Brevier der kulturbewussten Bürgerschaft, zu einem Element der Bewahrung des genius loci [...]. Nachgeborene verinnerlichten mit seiner Hilfe Bauten und städtebauliche Räume in der Vorstellung, obwohl sie diese nie erlebt hatten."[4] Wenn heute vom „Elbflorenz" die Rede ist, so wird *Das alte Dresden* vielleicht nicht immer mitgedacht, gemeint ist es dennoch, da sich darin jene Vergangenheit finden lässt, auf die so vielfältig Bezug genommen wird. Die Bedeutung des Buches lässt sich auch daran ermessen, in welchem Maße es Eingang in eine alternative Geschichtsschreibung im Sinne der Belletristik gefunden hat. Erwähnt wird es u. a. in Uwe Tellkamps Roman *Der Turm*, und auch für den Schriftsteller Ingo Schulze war es von außerordentlicher Bedeutung, wie er in seinem Essay *Ich war ein begeisterter Dresdner* darlegte: „Wir besaßen und hüteten eine relativ frühe Ausgabe von Fritz Löfflers *Das alte Dresden*, das mit seinem schwarzen Einband und der goldenen Schrift das eigentliche heilige Buch zu Hause

Bernardo Bellotto, genannt Canaletto, *Dresden vom rechten Elbufer unterhalb der Augustusbrücke*, 1748, Öl auf Leinwand, Gemäldegalerie Alte Meister, Dresden. —— Bernardo Bellotto, known as Canaletto, *Dresden from the Right Bank of the Elbe below the Augustus Bridge*, 1748, oil on canvas, Old Masters Gallery, Dresden.

intended as a posthumous eulogy to the city that was destroyed in 1945, the book became a guide for culturally conscious citizens, a way to safeguard the *genius loci* [...]. With his [Löffler's] help, later generations were able to internalise buildings and urban spaces in their imaginations, even though they had never seen them firsthand.'[4] When we speak of the 'Florence on the Elbe' today, it may not be with *Das alte Dresden* in mind, and yet it must always be an allusion to this work, which embodies the past so often referenced in this way. The book's significance can also be gauged by the extent to which it has become a part of the alternative history presented in fiction. It is mentioned, for instance, in Uwe Tellkamp's novel *Der Turm* (The Tower) and also played a significant role for the author Ingo Schulze, as Schulze himself describes in his essay 'Ich war ein begeisterter Dresdner' (I Was an Enthusiastic Dresdner): 'We owned and treasured a relatively early edition of Fritz Löffler's *Das alte Dresden*, which, with its black binding and gold lettering, was the actual holy book in our home.

war. Es hatte die Bedeutung eines Reliquiars, eines Stammbaums."[5] ——— Der Stammbaum, von dem Schulze spricht, reicht bis in das frühe Mittelalter zurück. Anziehend war der Elbtalkessel wohl vor allem deshalb, weil eine Furt die Überquerung des Flusses ermöglichte. Dementsprechend verweist der altsorbische Begriff „Drežďany" auch auf Sumpf- bzw. Auwaldbewohner. Die Ersterwähnung datiert auf das Jahr 1206, doch es wird bis zur Mitte des 16. Jahrhunderts dauern, ehe die linkselbische Siedlung und das rechtselbische Altendresden als zusammenhängendes Stadtgebiet aufgefasst werden. ——— Damals war der Herrschaftsbereich der regierenden Wettiner bereits im Zuge der Leipziger Teilung den Brüdern Ernst und Albrecht zugeschlagen worden. Als neuer Stammsitz der albertinischen Linie wurde Dresden zum Mittelpunkt des politischen, geistigen und kulturellen Lebens der Region. Das Residenzschloss geht in seiner Formgebung zumindest partiell auf diese Zeit zurück. Nachdem sich Heinrich der Fromme 1536 zur lutherischen Glaubenslehre bekannt hatte, wurde die Stadt zudem ein Zentrum des sächsischen Protestantismus. Nichtsdestotrotz überstand sie den Dreißigjährigen Krieg ohne größere Schäden, auch wenn die Entwicklung durch ausbleibenden Handel, Abgaben an Soldaten und grassierende Seuchen selbstredend erheblich beeinträchtigt wurde. ——— Unter Friedrich August I. – ab 1697 zudem als August II. König von Sachsen-Polen – stieg Dresden zur prunkvollen Elbmetropole auf. Seine Sonderstellung als absolutistischer Herrscher suchte er durch die Errichtung prestigeträchtiger Bauwerke in barockem Stil zu unterstreichen. Nach seinem Tod wurde rechts der Elbe ein goldenes Reiterstandbild platziert – unter August dem Starken war das 1685 abgebrannte Altendresden als Neustadt wieder aufgebaut worden. ——— Wenn dieser Tage an der Elbe Vergleiche mit der Hauptstadt der Toskana angestellt werden, dann ist dies ein Zeugnis italienischer Einflüsse im Augusteischen Zeitalter. „Vor allem aber sind es die Kunst- und Alterthumssammlungen, die er mit ansehnlichen Kosten stiftete, Trophäen seiner Regierung", schrieb Johann Gottfried Herder. „Was ein Friedrich August im Anfange des

It was as important as a reliquary or a family tree.'[5] ——— The family tree mentioned by Schulze reaches back to the early Middle Ages. Settlers were most likely drawn to the Dresden Basin because a ford made it possible to cross the Elbe River. Thus, the old Sorbian term 'Drežďany' is a reference to the residents of the marshes and riverside forest. The earliest use of the term dates to the year 1206, but the settlement on the left bank of the river and that of Altendresden on the right bank were not regarded as a connected municipality until the mid-sixteenth century. ——— At that time, the territory of the ruling House of Wettin had already been divided among the brothers Ernest and Albert as part of the Treaty of Leipzig. As the new ancestral seat of the Albertine line, Dresden was the heart of the region's political, intellectual, and cultural life. The design of the Royal Palace can be traced at least in part to this period. After Henry the Pious (Henry IV, Duke of Saxony) had converted to Lutheranism in 1536, the city also became a centre of Protestantism in Saxony. Nonetheless, it managed to survive the Thirty Years' War without sustaining any lasting damage, even if its development was, of course, severely impacted by the lack of trade, the payments made to soldiers, and rampant epidemics. ——— Dresden became a splendid metropolis on the Elbe River under the rule of Frederick Augustus I, Elector of Saxony (as of 1697, also Augustus II King of Saxony-Poland), who sought to underscore his position as absolute sovereign by building prestigious Baroque-style structures. After his death, a golden statue of a horseman was erected in his honour on the right bank of the Elbe River. Under Augustus the Strong, as he was known, Altendresden was rebuilt as a new town after being destroyed by a fire in 1685. ——— Present-day comparisons of Dresden to the Tuscan capital are a testimony to the Italian influence during the Augustan era. 'But the trophies of his reign are, above all, the collections of artworks and antiquities that he donated at a considerable cost', wrote Johann Gottfried Herder. 'What one Frederick Augustus began at the start of the century was completed by another [...] at century's end. Thanks to them, Dresden became a German Florence

Jahrhunderts anfing, hat ein anderer […] am Ende desselben vollendet. Durch sie ist Dresden in Ansehung der Kunstschätze ein Deutsches Florenz geworden."[6] —————— Friedrich August II. führte das städtebauliche Projekt seines Vaters fort – in seiner Regierungszeit entstanden u. a. die „Brühlschen Herrlichkeiten" am Terrassenufer – und trieb die Förderung der schönen Künste weiter voran. Großen Einfluss hatte seine Vorliebe für das Singspiel, das Opernhaus am Zwinger stieg unter seiner Ägide zu einem der bedeutendsten Theater Europas auf und ist als Vorläufer der Semperoper zu sehen. Als leidenschaftlicher Kunstsammler gelang es ihm, beispielsweise die *Sixtinische Madonna* von Raffael zu erwerben, jenes Werk, das heute in der Galerie Alte Meister eine Sonderstellung einnimmt. Der „Canaletto" genannte venezianische Maler Bernardo Bellotto schuf am kurfürstlichen Hof Stadtansichten, die die Wahrnehmung der Stadt bis in die Gegenwart beeinflussen. —————— Bereits 1768 war die Gemäldesammlung so berühmt, dass sie den jungen Goethe zu einer Reise nach Dresden bewegte. Doch eindrücklicher als die Kunst erschien dem Dichter der Zustand der Stadt, wie er in seiner Autobiografie *Aus meinem Leben. Dichtung und Wahrheit* festhielt: „Diese köstlichen, Geist und Sinn zur wahren Kunst vorbereitenden Erfahrungen wurden jedoch durch einen der traurigsten Anblicke unterbrochen und gedämpft, durch den zerstörten und verödeten Zustand so mancher Straße Dresdens, durch die ich meinen Weg nahm […]. Von der Kuppel der Frauenkirche sah ich diese leidigen Trümmern zwischen die schöne städtische Ordnung hineingesät."[7] Was Goethe vorgefunden hatte, war das Resultat eines Bombardements im Siebenjährigen Krieg, die Festung an der Elbe hatte im Mittelpunkt schwerer Auseinandersetzungen zwischen den Preußen unter Friedrich dem Großen und dem Kaiserlichen Heer gestanden. —————— Mit Friedrich Schiller stattete ein anderer bedeutender Vertreter der Weimarer Klassik Dresden einen Besuch ab. In einem Häuschen auf einem Weinberg in Loschwitz vollendete er die *Ode An die Freude*, die Ludwig van Beethoven später als Textgrundlage für seine 9. Sinfonie verwenden sollte. —————— Etwas weiter stromauf-

Hyacinthe Rigaud, *Bildnis König Augusts II. von Polen*, Öl auf Leinwand, Musée cantonal des Beaux-Arts, Lausanne. —————— Hyacinthe Rigaud, *Portrait of King Augustus II of Poland*, oil on canvas, Musée cantonal des Beaux-Arts, Lausanne.

in respect of artistic treasures.'[6] —————— Frederick Augustus II continued his father's project of urban development ('Brühl's Glories', for example, were created along the shore of the Elbe River during his reign). He also promoted the fine arts, in which his passion for musical theatre was a driving influence. The Zwinger Palace Opera House became one of the most important theatres in Europe thanks to his support and was the forerunner to the Semper Opera. As an avid art collector, he was able to acquire the *Sistine Madonna* by Raphael, a work that holds a special position in the Gallery of Old Masters today. At the royal court, the Venetian artist Bernardo Bellotto, known as 'Canaletto', painted views of Dresden that still influence present-day perceptions of the city. —————— In 1768, this collection of paintings was already so famous that it prompted the young Johann Wolfgang von Goethe to travel to Dresden. However, the condition of the city

wärts wurde 1791 Geschichte geschrieben. In Reaktion auf die Französische Revolution sicherten Österreich und Preußen während einer Fürstenversammlung Ludwig XVI. ihre Unterstützung zu. Mit der Pillnitzer Deklaration spitzte sich die politische Lage in Europa zu. In den Koalitionskriegen kämpfte Kursachsen zunächst an der Seite Preußens, trat 1806 jedoch dem Rheinbund bei. Die entscheidende Schlacht, die das Ende der Vorherrschaft Napoleons in deutschen Landen einleiten sollte, fand bei Leipzig statt. ——————— Nach den Befreiungskriegen wurden die Festungswerke zurückgebaut, dadurch zum Beispiel die Brühlsche Terrasse für die Öffentlichkeit zugänglich gemacht. In der Folge wurden auch im Deutschen Bund liberale Forderungen laut. Die Märzrevolution kulminierte in Sachsen im Dresdner Maiaufstand, der von der Restauration niedergeschlagen wurde. Zu den Aufrührern gehörten auch der Architekt Gottfried Semper sowie der damalige Hofkapellmeister Richard Wagner. Beide mussten aus der Stadt fliehen. ——————— Zur Etablierung des „Mythos Dresden", den Löffler zu bewahren suchte, trugen zahlreiche Künstler bei, die im 19. Jahrhundert in der Stadt gewirkt haben. So hinterließen etwa Carl Maria von Weber und Robert Schumann, Caspar David Friedrich und Ludwig Richter, aber auch Heinrich von Kleist und Ludwig Tieck ihre Spuren. „Am Himmelfahrtstage, Nachmittags um drei Uhr, rannte ein junger Mensch in Dresden durchs Schwarze Thor"[8] – mit der Novelle *Der goldene Topf* von E. T. A. Hoffmann spielt gar ein zentrales Werk der deutschen Romantik an der Elbe. ——————— Der Aufstieg des Bürgertums war, nicht zuletzt durch die einsetzende Industrialisierung begünstigt, bald nicht mehr aufzuhalten. Die Novemberrevolution besiegelte schließlich das Ende der Monarchie in Sachsen. Dresden, die Hauptstadt des Freistaates, war mit mehr als einer halben Million Einwohner die sechstgrößte Stadt der Weimarer Republik, wirtschaftliches Schwergewicht und – da die Fronten des Ersten Weltkriegs weit entfernt verlaufen waren – ein städtebauliches Glanzstück.

made a greater impression on the writer than did the art therein, as he wrote in his autobiography *Aus meinem Leben. Dichtung und Wahrheit* (translated as *Truth and Fiction Relating to My Life*): 'These delightful experiences, preparing both mind and sense for true art, were nevertheless interrupted and damped by one of the most melancholy sights,—by the destroyed and desolate condition of so many of the streets of Dresden through which I took my way. [...] From the cupola of the Church of Our Lady (*Frauenkirche*) I saw these pitiable ruins scattered about amid the beautiful order of the city.'[7] What Goethe had seen was the result of sustained military fire during the Seven Years' War. The stronghold on the Elbe River had been at the centre of intense fighting between the imperial army and the Prussians under the command of Frederick the Great. ——————— Friedrich Schiller was another important representative of Weimar Classicism who visited Dresden. He completed his 'Ode to Joy', later used as the textual basis for Ludwig van Beethoven's 'Ninth Symphony', in a little cottage on a vineyard in Loschwitz. ——————— A little further upstream, history was written in 1791. In reaction to the French Revolution, Austria and Prussia assured Louis XVI of their support during an assembly of sovereign princes. The resulting Pillnitz Declaration aggravated the political climate in Europe. The Electorate of Saxony, which had initially fought alongside Prussia in the Coalition Wars, joined the Confederation of the Rhine in 1806. The decisive battle that was supposed to bring an end to Napoleon's dominance of German territories was fought near Leipzig. ——————— After the Wars of Liberation, the fortifications were dismantled, making Brühl's Terrace, for instance, accessible to the public. Liberal demands also became more forceful in the German Confederation. In Saxony, the March Revolution of 1848 culminated in the May Uprising in Dresden, which was defeated by the Restoration. Among the rebels were the architect Gottfried Semper and Richard Wagner the court conductor at the time. Both men were forced to flee the city. ——————— Several nineteenth-century artists contributed to the 'Myth of Dresden' that Löffler tried to preserve. Carl Maria von

DIE ZERSTÖRUNG DRESDENS

Ich sah Bilder der Dresdener Nacht vor mir,
ich dachte immerfort den einen Satz: die Fittiche
des Todes rauschen, es ist keine Phrase,
die Fittiche des Todes rauschen wirklich.

Victor Klemperer[9]

1920 erhielt Victor Klemperer einen Lehrstuhl an der Technischen Hochschule Dresden. Seine Tagebücher gelten als eines der wichtigsten Zeugnisse der systematischen Judenverfolgung im Dritten Reich. „Die Judenhetze ist maßlos geworden, weit schlimmer als beim ersten Boykott", notierte der Professor für Romanistik bereits im August 1935. „Pogromanfänge gibt es da und dort, und wir rechnen damit, hier nächstens totgeschlagen zu werden. Nicht durch Nachbarn, aber durch Nettoyeurs, die man da und dort als Volksseele einsetzt. An den Straßenbahnschildern der Prager Straße: Wer beim Juden kauft, ist ein Volksverräter."[10] ——— Als die Pogrome, von denen Klemperer schreibt, im November 1938 einen vorläufigen Höhepunkt erreichten, ging die Dresdner Synagoge – ebenfalls von Gottfried Semper entworfen – in Flammen auf. In der Folge kam es zu ersten Deportationen. Die verbliebenen Juden, darunter auch Klemperer, wurden in als „Judenhäuser" bezeichneten Unterkünften untergebracht – Luftschutzräume durften sie nicht betreten. Gab es 1933 noch 5000 Gemeindemitglieder in der Stadt, sollten nur ca. 70 Dresdner Juden dem Holocaust entkommen. ——— Die Nationalsozialisten gingen nicht nur gegen in ihren Augen „lebensunwertes Leben", sondern auch gegen Vertreter eines vermeintlich „undeutschen Geistes" vor. Werke verfemter Autoren wurden bei inszenierten Veranstaltungen ins Feuer geworfen. Der gebürtige Dresdner Erich Kästner wohnte einer u.a. gegen ihn gerichteten Aktion persönlich bei: „Und im Jahre 1933 wurden meine Bücher in Berlin, auf dem großen Platz neben der Staatsoper, von einem gewissen Herrn Goebbels mit düster feierlichem Pomp verbrannt", berichtete er in *Bei Durchsicht meiner Bücher*, dem ersten Buch, das nach dem Krieg wieder in Deutsch-

Weber and Robert Schumann, Caspar David Friedrich and Ludwig Richter, Heinrich von Kleist and Ludwig Tieck—they all left their mark on the city. With E.T.A. Hoffmann's novella *Der goldene Topf* (translated as *The Golden Flower Pot*), a central work of German Romanticism is set in this city on the Elbe: 'On Ascension Day, about three o'clock in the afternoon in Dresden, a young man dashed through the [...] Black Gate.'[8] ——— The rise of the middle class could soon no longer be stopped, due in no small part to the advent of industrialisation. The November Revolution ultimately brought an end to the monarchy in Saxony. With more than half a million residents, Dresden, the capital of the Free State of Saxony, was the sixth largest city in the Weimar Republic, an economic heavyweight, and (since far removed from the frontlines of the First World War) an architectural gem.

DRESDEN'S DESTRUCTION

My vision swam with images of the night on which Dresden was bombed,
the whole time, I was thinking: the wings
of death are beating, it's not a cliché,
the wings of death are really beating.

Victor Klemperer[9]

In 1920, Victor Klemperer obtained a professorship at the Technical University of Dresden. His diaries are considered some of the most important accounts of the systematic persecution of Jews that followed. 'The attacks on Jews have grown boundless, far worse than during the first boycott', the Professor of Romance Languages noted as early as August 1935. 'The first signs of a pogrom can be seen here and there, and we expect to be beaten to death before too long. Not by our neighbours, but by the *nettoyeurs* who are being employed here and there to represent the soul of the nation. The tram signs on Prager Strasse read, 'Anyone who buys from Jews is a traitor.'[10] ——— As the pogroms described by Klemperer reached their preliminary climax in

Louis Thümling, *Alte Dresdner Synagoge*, 1860, Lithografie. —— Louis Thümling, *Old Dresden Synagogue*, 1860, lithograph.

land erschien. „Vierundzwanzig deutsche Schriftsteller, die symbolisch für immer ausgetilgt werden sollten, rief er triumphierend beim Namen. Ich war der einzige der Vierundzwanzig, der persönlich erschienen war, um dieser theatralischen Frechheit beizuwohnen."[11] —— Noch im selben Jahr wurde im Neuen Rathaus die Ausstellung *Entartete Kunst* eröffnet. Dresden war am Beginn des 20. Jahrhunderts zu einem Epizentrum des Expressionismus geworden – wovon zum Beispiel die Künstlergruppe *Brücke* sowie die *Dresdner Sezession* Ausdruck gaben. Nun wurden Ernst Ludwig Kirchner, Otto Dix, Oskar Kokoschka – vormals Professor an der städtischen Kunstakademie – und viele andere gebrandmarkt. Von der Elbe ging die diffamierende Sammlung auf Wanderschaft, ehe sie 1937 in die gleichnamige Propagandaausstellung in München integriert wurde. —— Die Zerstörung der Kleinstadt Wieluń durch die Luftwaffe im Zuge des Überfalls auf Polen gilt als erste Militäraktion des Zweiten Weltkriegs. Mehr als je zuvor strebten die Konfliktparteien die Dominanz über den Luftraum an. Während des Westfeldzuges geriet schließlich auch das Vereinigte Königreich ins Visier deutscher Bomber. Dabei wurde u. a. Coventry – heute Partnerstadt Dresdens – schwer beschädigt. „The Blitz" zeigte den Briten, wie mit großflächigen Abwürfen ein verheerender Feuersturm entfacht werden konnte. Im Februar 1942 wurde Arthur Harris, dem Oberkommandieren-

November 1938, Dresden's synagogues (also designed by Gottfried Semper) went up in flames. The first deportations began after that. The remaining Jews, Klemperer among them, were moved into buildings known as 'Jew houses' and were not permitted to enter air-raid shelters. In 1933, the city's Jewish community had numbered five thousand, but only seventy or so of Dresden's Jews survived the Holocaust. —— The National Socialists were taking action not only against what they considered 'lives not worthy of life' but also against the representatives of a supposed 'un-German spirit'. During staged events, they burned the works of banned authors. Erich Kästner, a Dresden native, personally attended one of these campaigns, at which he was one of the authors being targeted. 'And in 1933, my books were burned with sombre ceremony by a certain Mr Goebbels, in the great square next to the State Opera in Berlin,' he reported in *Bei Durchsicht meiner Bücher* (Upon Looking Through My Books), the first of his books to be published again in Germany after the war. 'Triumphantly, he called out the names of twenty-four German authors, whose works were supposed to be symbolically eradicated. I was the only one of the twenty-four who had appeared in person to witness this theatrical effrontery.'[11] —— That same year, the exhibition titled *Entartete Kunst* (Degenerate Art) was opened at the New Town Hall. Dresden had become the epicentre of Expressionism in the early twentieth century, as was seen in the work of the artists' groups *Die Brücke* (The Bridge) and *Dresdner Sezession* (Dresden Secession). Now, Ernst Ludwig Kirchner, Otto Dix, Oskar Kokoschka—a former professor at Dresden's Art Academy—and many others were being stigmatized. The defamatory collection travelled from the Elbe to other parts of the country before being included in the propagandistic exhibition of the same name in Munich in 1937. —— The destruction of the town of Wieluń by the *Luftwaffe* during Germany's invasion of Poland is considered the first military campaign of the Second World War. More than ever before, the warring factions now battled to gain dominance over the skies. During the invasion of

den des Bomber Command der Royal Air Force, vom Air Ministry die Erlaubnis zum „moral bombing" erteilt, zu Angriffen, die die Zivilbevölkerung entmutigen sollen. ———— Da Dresden sich zunächst außerhalb des Aktionsradius alliierter Bomber befand, blieb das Elbtal allerdings bis in den Herbst 1944 praktisch verschont. Doch die kommunalen Bahnhöfe bildeten zu jener Zeit einen bedeutenden Knotenpunkt im Streckennetz der Deutschen Reichsbahn. Die Industrie der Region war nahezu vollständig auf die Produktion von Rüstungsgütern umgestellt worden. Zudem galt die Stadt als wichtiger Versorgungsposten hinter der Ostfront – und Vorbereitungen, den Elbübergang mit einer Festung zu sichern, waren bereits in vollem Gange. So rückte Dresden in den Fokus der Luftstreitkräfte. ———— Der in deutsche Kriegsgefangenschaft geratene US-Soldat Kurt Vonnegut erlebte die fatalen Angriffe auf dem Gelände des Städtischen Viehbetriebs im Großen Ostragehege. In seinem später erschienenen Roman *Schlachthof 5 oder Der Kinderkreuzzug* verarbeitete er seine Erlebnisse: „Er war unten in dem Fleischkeller in jener Nacht, als Dresden zerstört wurde. Oben waren Geräusche wie von riesigen Schritten. Es waren Reiheneinschläge hochexplosiver Bomben. Die Riesen schritten und schritten. Der Fleischkeller war ein sehr sicherer Unterstand. Alles, was dort unten geschah, war ein gelegentlicher Schauer von Kalkbewurf."[12] ———— Eine sichere Zuflucht suchen viele Dresdner zwischen dem 13. und dem 15. Februar 1945 vergeblich. 174 Mal war zuvor bereits in der Stadt Fliegeralarm ertönt. Spätestens nachdem die Alliierten die Luftüberlegenheit erlangt hatten, waren Vorkehrungen für einen Militärschlag getroffen worden. Um die faschistische

France, the United Kingdom also ultimately became the target of German bombers. Coventry—today, Dresden's twin city—was one of the sites that were badly damaged during the attack. 'The Blitz' showed the British how a devastating firestorm could be ignited by the large-scale dropping of bombs. In February 1942, the Air Ministry authorised Arthur Harris, the commander-in-chief of the Royal Air Force Bomber Command, to conduct 'moral bombings', attacks intended to demoralise the civilian population. ———— Since Dresden initially fell outside the radius of Allied bombing campaigns, the Elbe Valley remained largely unscathed until the autumn of 1944. At this time, however, the municipal railway stations constituted an important junction in the network of the German Reichsbahn (National Railway), and the industry in the region had shifted almost entirely to the production of armaments. In addition, the city was considered an important supply post behind the eastern front, and preparations for securing the Elbe crossing with a fortification were in full swing. Thus, Dresden drew the attention of Allied air forces. ———— Kurt Vonnegut, a U.S. soldier captured by the Germans, experienced the fatal attacks while being held on the city's livestock holding grounds in the area known as Grosses Ostragehege. He drew on these events in his later novel *Slaughterhouse-Five, Or the Children's Crusade*: 'He was down in the meat locker on the night that Dresden was destroyed. There were sounds

Kriegsmaschinerie nicht ins Stocken geraten zu lassen, war allerdings auf den Bau von Bunkern weitgehend verzichtet worden. ——— Zunächst werfen britische Bomber Luftminen sowie Sprengbomben ab, um die Häuser abzudecken. Die Bevölkerung flieht in die Keller, so auch der Maler Otto Griebel: „Ein vielfaches Pfeifen durchschnitt die Luft, und dann erzitterte das Haus von einer Reihe rasch aufeinander erfolgender und immer heftiger werdender Detonationen, die uns in eine Ecke des Kellers trieben […]. Wir duckten uns immer tiefer und warteten von einem Hieb zum anderen. Einmal schien es, als drehe sich das ganze Gebäude in seinen Fundamenten. Dann

Die Schrecken des Krieges 1945 in Dresden. So geht das. —— The horrors of war: 1945 in Dresden. So it goes.

brach rote Lohe durch die Kellerlöcher."[13] ——— In einem zweiten Schlag bringen Bomber der Royal Air Force Stabbrandbomben über dem Zielgebiet zum Abwurf. Aus den zahlreichen Feuern entwickelt sich ein Flächenbrand, dem kaum zu entkommen ist, wie Klemperer in *LTI*, seiner berühmten Analyse des faschistischen Wortgebrauchs, festhielt: „Am Abend dieses 13. Februar brach die Katastrophe über Dresden herein: die Bomben fielen, die Häuser stürzten, der Phosphor strömte, die brennenden Balken krachten auf arische und nichtarische Köpfe, und derselbe Feuersturm riß Jud und Christ in den Tod."[14] ——— Bei Tagesanbruch erweist sich das Zentrum der Stadt

like giant footsteps above. Those were sticks of high-explosive bombs. The giants walked and walked. The meat locker was a very safe shelter. All that happened down there was an occasional shower of calcimine.'[12] ——— Many of Dresden's residents were not fortunate enough to find a safe refuge between 13 and 15 February 1945. Prior to this, the city's air raid sirens had already sounded 174 times. Once the Allied forces had achieved air superiority, it was not long before they began preparing a military attack. However, rather than allow the fascist war-machine to come to a halt, the German government had largely abstained from building bunkers. ——— To begin with, British bombers dropped aerial mines and explosive bombs that covered entire residential areas. The city's population sought shelter in basements; the painter Otto Griebel, for instance, remembers: 'Frequent whistling sounds cut through the air, and then the house was shaken by a series of detonations that followed one after the other in quick succession and with increasing force, driving us into a corner of the basement […]. We huddled lower and lower and waited from one strike to the next. At one point, it felt as if the entire building was turning on its foundation. Then red flames broke through the cracks in the basement.'[13] ——— In a second attack, the bombers of the Royal Air Force dropped stick-type incendiary bombs over target areas, and the numerous fires developed into a conflagration that was nearly impossible to escape. Klemperer describes the night of this attack in *LTI* (translated as *The Language of the Third Reich: A Philologist's Notebook*), his famous analysis of the fascist use of language: 'On the evening of 13 February that year, catastrophe descended upon Dresden: the bombs fell, houses collapsed, phosphorus poured forth, the burning rafters crashed upon Aryan and non-Aryan heads alike, and both Jews and Christians lost their lives in the same firestorm.'[14] ——— At daybreak, the city centre was revealed to be impassable; streets, tram lines, and railway tracks were destroyed. Nevertheless, thousands of people pushed their way out of the city. 'The stream of refugees made its way along a main road behind the

als unpassierbar, Straßen, Tramtrassen wie Eisenbahnschienen sind zerstört. Dennoch drängen Tausende Menschen aus der Stadt. „Der Flüchtlingsstrom ging an einer Ausfallstraße hinter dem zerbombten Bahnhofsgelände entlang", berichtete die Komponistin Aleida Montijn in ihrer Biografie. „Es muß gegen 12 Uhr Mittags gewesen sein, als der dritte Angriff auf Dresden begann. Ich entsinne mich an einen rechts von der Landstraße gelegenen Stollen, der überfüllt war von Menschen, die schon dorthinein geflüchtet waren, als man das dumpfe Dröhnen der herannahenden Bomberpulks hörte."[15] Diesmal sind es Maschinen der United States Army Air Force, die Dresden anfliegen. ——— Am 15. Februar kehren die Amerikaner noch einmal zurück, es wird der vierte und letzte Luftschlag einer Angriffsserie, die heutzutage gemeinhin als „Zerstörung Dresdens" bezeichnet wird. Kurz bevor zum wiederholten Mal Bomben niedergehen, stürzt als letztes Gebäude am Neumarkt die Frauenkirche ein. Zahlreiche weitere Kulturstätten und Denkmäler sind zerstört, aber erst in den folgenden Tagen zeichnet sich das Ausmaß der Verwüstung ab. Der Wohnraum in den betroffenen Stadtteilen liegt nahezu vollständig in Trümmern. Die Fabriken sind schwer getroffen. Zehntausende Menschen haben den Tod gefunden. Es ist eines der schwersten Flächenbombardements des Zweiten Weltkriegs. „Dresden war jetzt wie der Mond", heißt es bei Vonnegut, „nichts als Mineralien. Die Steine waren heiß. Alle anderen im weiteren Umkreis waren tot. So geht das."[16] ——— Nichtsdestotrotz wurde bald darauf die Befestigung der Stadt wieder aufgenommen. Dresden, so der Befehl, sollte gehalten werden bis zum Letzten. Zwei Monate später kam es flussabwärts zum „Handschlag von Torgau", dem ersten Aufeinandertreffen von amerikanischen und sowjetischen Truppen auf deutschem Boden. Am 8. Mai 1945 ging mit der Kapitulation der Wehrmacht der Zweite Weltkrieg in Europa zu Ende. Dresden war bis dahin noch von weiteren Luftangriffen erschüttert worden, doch den Schlusspunkt hatten faschistische Streitkräfte gesetzt: Am Vortag waren, die anrückende Rote Armee im Blick, die Albert-, die Carola- und die Augustusbrücke gesprengt worden.

„Wie liegt die Stadt so wüst": Dresden nach den Angriffen der Alliierten. ——— 'How desolate is the city': Dresden after the attacks by Allied forces.

bombed railway station', the composer Aleida Montijn reports in her biography. 'It must have been around noon when the third attack on Dresden began. I remember an underground tunnel to the right of the road was packed with people who had taken shelter there as soon as they heard the dull drone of the approaching swarm of bombers.'[15] This time, Dresden was the target of the United States Air Force. ——— The Americans returned on 15 February, the day of the fourth and final air strike in a series of attacks commonly referred to as 'Dresden's Destruction'. Shortly before the bombs rained down yet again, the last remaining building at the Neumarkt square, the *Frauenkirche* or Church of Our Lady, also collapsed. Numerous other cultural sites and monuments had been destroyed as well. The extent of the devastation became clear in the days that followed. The residential areas in the bombed districts of the city were almost completely reduced to rubble. The factories had been badly hit. Tens of thousands of people had been killed in one of the worst carpet-bombing attacks of the

MYTHOS DRESDEN

> Wenn es einen Mythos Dresden gab, dann war
> sein Herz die Ruine der Frauenkirche.
>
> Ingo Schulze[17]

Im Zuge einer Verwaltungsreform im Jahr 1952 wurde
Dresden zum Zentrum des neu geschaffenen Bezirks
gleichen Namens. Zu diesem Zeitpunkt war die Stadt
bereits größtenteils enttrümmert. Während zahlreiche
historische Wohngebäude aus dem Stadtbild ver-
schwanden, wurden repräsentative Bauwerke wie
etwa der Zwinger, die Kreuzkirche oder das Opernhaus
rekonstruiert – wenngleich bis zur Wiederherstellung
teilweise Jahrzehnte vergehen sollten. Dem Abriss
markanter Architektur gingen – in erster Linie ist hier
die Sophienkirche beim Postplatz zu nennen – heftige
Proteste voraus. ——— Noch heute lassen sich in
Dresden divergierende Phasen ostdeutscher Stadt-
planung nachvollziehen. Wurden beim Komplex an
der Ecke Altmarkt, Wilsdruffer Straße noch die im *Auf-
baugesetz* verankerten *16 Grundsätze des Städtebaus*
verfolgt, spielten die Vorgaben des Sozialistischen
Klassizismus beim später errichteten Kulturpalast keine Rolle mehr. Ab 1969 wechselten am Platz historisierend den Dresdner Barock aufgreifende Fassaden
mit einem modernistischen, quaderförmigen Solitär.
Für die Gestaltung einer Fußgängerzone auf den nach
dem Krieg in Gänze abgetragenen Flächen an der
Prager Straße wurde in großem Maße auf Plattenbauweise zurückgegriffen. ——— 1989 richteten sich
die Augen der Weltöffentlichkeit auf die westdeut-
sche Botschaft in Prag. Tausende DDR-Bürger hatten
das Gelände besetzt, um eine Ausreise in die Bundes-
republik Deutschland zu erwirken. Nach der Zustim-
mung wurden die eingesetzten Sonderzüge u. a. durch
Dresden geführt. Am Hauptbahnhof hinderten Sicher-
heitskräfte Ausreisewillige gewaltsam daran, bei der
Durchfahrt aufzuspringen. ——— Als Schlüsselmo-
ment der politischen Wende erscheint im Nachhinein
eine Rede des damaligen Bundeskanzlers im Dezem-
ber jenes Jahres. „Und auch das, lassen Sie mich hier
auf diesem traditionsreichen Platz sagen", leitete Hel-

Second World War. 'Dresden was like the moon now',
Vonnegut writes, 'nothing but minerals. The stones
were hot. Everybody else in the neighbourhood was
dead. So it goes.'[16] ——— Nonetheless, the fortification of the city was resumed soon after. The orders
were clear: Dresden should be held until the very
end. Further downstream, the famous 'Handshake of
Torgau' took place two months later, when American
and Soviet troops met for the first time on German
soil. On 8 May 1945, the German Wehrmacht surren-
dered, bringing an end to the Second World War in
Europe. Dresden had been shaken by additional air
strikes prior to this, but the final blow had been dealt
by the fascists themselves: with the Red Army closing
in, the Albert, Carola, and Augustus bridges had been
demolished just one day before the end of the war.

THE MYTH OF DRESDEN

> If there was such a thing as the myth of Dresden,
> then the ruins of the Church of Our Lady were at its
> heart.
>
> Ingo Schulze[17]

During the course of administrative reforms in 1952,
Dresden became the centre of the newly created district of the same name. The city had largely been
cleared of rubble by this time. Several historical resi-
dences disappeared from the cityscape altogether,
but representative structures such as the Zwinger
Palace, the Kreuzkirche or Church of the Holy Cross,
and the opera house were reconstructed (though their
restoration sometimes took decades to complete).
The demolition of prominent architectural works—
specifically, the Sophienkirche or Saint Sophia's Church
located at Postplatz—gave rise to fierce protests.
——— The divergent phases of East German city
planning can still be seen in Dresden today. Whereas
the design of the building complex at the corner of
Altmarkt square and Wilsdruffer Strasse still followed
the *Sixteen Principles of City Planning* laid down in the
Construction Act, the standards of Socialist Classicism

mut Kohl damals seine elementare Botschaft ein. „Mein Ziel bleibt – wenn die geschichtliche Stunde es zulässt – die Einheit unserer Nation."[18] Er sprach auf dem Neumarkt zu etwa 100 000 Menschen. ——— „Freilich ist der Bundeskanzler als solcher vor lauter Menschen gar nicht zu sehen, aber seine Stimme direkt über uns", erinnerte sich Thomas Rosenlöcher in seinem Dresdner Tagebuch *Die verkauften Pflastersteine* an den Auftritt. „Von weit da vorn kommt sie, wo das Scheinwerferlicht die Frauenkirchenruine mit ihren beiden Stümpfen und dem Geröllberg in ein fernes Mysterium aus weißflüssigem Silber verwandelt hat."[19] ——— Nach der Wiedervereinigung setzte in der Hauptstadt des neuen Bundeslandes Sachsen der Wiederaufbau der barocken Altstadt ein. Angesichts der zahlreichen Baustellen sprach man in Anlehnung an Bellottos populäre Gemälde spöttisch vom „Krahnaletto-Blick". Den historisierenden Neubauten wurde mitunter kritisch begegnet, gerade die Rekonstruktion des Vergangenen, so ein gängiges Argument, würde die geschichtliche Entwicklung der Stadt verwischen. Im Mittelpunkt der Auseinandersetzungen stand die Errichtung einer „neuen" Frauenkirche, dem Bauwerk, das den Mythos Dresden wie kein zweites verkörperte. Sie war zu DDR-Zeiten als Mahnmal des Krieges im zerstörten Zustand belassen worden. ——— Noch bevor am Neumarkt der Weihegottesdienst stattfinden konnte, hatte die UNESCO das Elbtal samt seiner kulturellen Schätze zum Welterbe erklärt. Mit dem Bau der Waldschlößchenbrücke wurde der Titel allerdings nur wenige Jahre darauf wieder aberkannt. Am umstrittenen Verkehrszug über die Elbe war es ein weiteres Mal zu Konflikten zwischen Bewahrern des alten Dresdens und Befürwortern moderner Stadtentwicklung gekommen. ——— Der Streit um die historische Einordnung der Luftangriffe war schon lange vorher entbrannt. So statteten bereits im März 1945 zwei Funktionäre der Gauleitung Gerhart Hauptmann einen Besuch ab. Der hochbetagte Schriftsteller hatte die Zerstörung der Stadt während eines Aufenthalts in einem Sanatorium in Wachwitz miterlebt und sollte Stellung beziehen. „Wer das Weinen verlernt hat, der lernt es wieder beim Un-

no longer played a role when the Kulturpalast (Palace of Culture) was built. From 1969 on, construction at the square alternated between historicising facades reminiscent of Dresden's Baroque architecture and distinctive modernist cuboid buildings. The creation of a pedestrian zone on Prager Strasse, the surface of which had been completely eroded after the war, relied heavily on the use of pre-fabricated concrete slabs. ——— In 1989, the eyes of world were trained on the West German embassy in Prague. Thousands of GDR citizens had occupied the premises in the hope of being able to emigrate to the Federal Republic of Germany. After permission was granted, the special trains used for this purpose also passed through Dresden. At the central railway station, security forces did not shy away from using violence to prevent prospective emigrants from jumping on the trains as they went by. ——— In retrospect, a speech given by the West German Chancellor in December of that year seems to represent a key moment of the political transition. 'And, here on this square so steeped in tradition, let me also say this', Helmut Kohl began in delivering his fundamental message. 'My goal remains—insofar as this historic hour allows it—the union of our nation.'[18] He was speaking to a crowd of approximately one-hundred thousand people gathered at Neumarkt square. 'Of course, we could not even see the Chancellor amid the masses of people, but his voice was directly above us', Thomas Rosenlöcher recalls of the event in his diary *Die verkauften Pflastersteine* (Sold Paving Stones). 'We heard it coming from far in front, where the spotlight shining on the ruins of the Church of Our Lady, with its two stumps and the mountain of rubble, had turned it into a distant mystery of white liquid silver.'[19] ——— After Germany's reunification, the capital of the new state of Saxony began the restoration of its Baroque historic centre. Given the large number of construction sites, people spoke of the 'Crane-aletto view' in mocking reference to Bellotto's popular paintings. The historicisation of new buildings was also met with criticism; a common argument held that, by reconstructing its past, the city was erasing its historical development.

tergang Dresdens. Dieser heitere Morgenstern der Jugend hat bisher der Welt geleuchtet."[20] Der Auftakt der verbreiteten Erklärung des Literaturnobelpreisträgers ist heute allseits bekannt – dass ein Abschnitt, der eine differenzierte Wahrnehmung der Kriegsgegner bewirken sollte, bei der Aufbereitung für Presse und Rundfunk gestrichen wurde, weniger: „Ich weiß, dass in England und Amerika gute Geister genug vorhanden sind, denen das göttliche Licht der Sixtinischen Madonna nicht fremd war und die von dem Erlöschen dieses Sternes allertiefst getroffen weinen." ——— In den wenigen Wochen bis zum Ende des Krieges gelang es der faschistischen Propaganda eine Interpretation der Ereignisse zu verbreiten, die die Rezeption bis in die Gegenwart beeinflusst. Die Angriffe wurden einerseits als skrupellose Vernichtungsfeldzüge gegen die Zivilbevölkerung deklariert, andererseits als barbarische Zerstörung einer militärisch unbedeutenden, dafür jedoch kulturell einzigartigen Großstadt. Wendungen wie „Bomber-Harris" oder „anglo-amerikanischer Luftterror" sind noch immer im Umlauf. Implizit wurde dadurch auf eine Relativierung der deutschen Kriegsschuld hingewirkt, andererseits der Opferstatus gestärkt. So wurde nicht etwa die von den Deutschen angezettelte Luftschlacht um England zum Symbol für die Zerstörungskraft des Bombenkrieges, sondern Dresden. ——— Die ohne Zweifel traumatisierenden Geschehnisse während der Bombardierung begünstigten die Legendenbildung. Augenzeugen – so auch Victor Klemperer, wie wir oben gesehen haben – berichteten von Phosphorbomben, über den Elbauen hätten Tiefflieger Flüchtende ins Visier genommen. Obgleich nie Belege erbracht werden konnten, haben die vermeintlichen Gräueltaten der Alliierten weite Verbreitung gefunden. Dies änderte sich auch in der Deutschen Demokratischen Republik nur teilweise. Zwar fanden nun die deutschen Kriegsverbrechen Beachtung, jedoch wurden im Kalten Krieg die Angriffe als Argument gegen den Imperialismus ins Feld geführt. ——— Wie viele Menschen starben in Dresden? Die Popularisierung vermeintlicher Opferzahlen kann beispielhaft für einen tendenziösen Umgang mit Daten und Fakten stehen. So war

At the centre of the debate was the creation of a 'new' Church of Our Lady, the edifice that embodied the myth of Dresden like no other. During the era of the GDR, it had been left in its ruined state as a memorial to the Second World War. ——— Even before the church's consecration service was held at Neumarkt square, the UNESCO had declared the Elbe Valley and its cultural treasures a world heritage site. A few years later, however, the title was revoked after the construction of the Waldschlösschen Bridge. This controversial road bridge across the Elbe River had once more led to conflicts between the preservers of Old Dresden and the promoters of modern city development. ——— The debate concerning how the air strikes on the city should be recorded in history had begun much earlier. In March 1945, for instance, two officials from the Nazi Party's regional administration visited Gerhart Hauptmann. The elderly author had witnessed the destruction of the city during his stay at a sanatorium in Wachwitz and was asked to give his opinion: 'Even someone who had forgotten how to cry would weep at the destruction of Dresden. Until now, this cheerful morning star of youth shone for all the world.'[20] This prelude to the Nobel laureate's explanation is familiar to many today; it is less well-known that a portion of his speech, which was intended to produce a more nuanced awareness in Germany's former wartime enemies, was omitted in the version revised for the press and radio: 'I know that there are plenty of benevolent souls in England and America who are not strangers to the divine light of the Sistine Madonna and who weep because they are deeply affected by the extinction of this star.' ——— In the few weeks before the end of the war, fascist propaganda was able to disseminate an interpretation of events that has influenced perceptions to the present day. On the one hand, the attacks were portrayed as ruthless campaigns of destruction against the civilian population and, on the other, as the barbaric destruction of a culturally unique city with little military significance. Expressions like 'Bomber Harris' or 'Anglo-American air terror' are still used today. Implicitly, such representations were intended to

zwar bereits 1966 im Koblenzer Bundesarchiv ein Dokument gefunden worden, das Manipulationen der faschistischen Führung offenbarte – die vermeldeten Werte für Tote und Verletzte waren schlicht um das Zehnfache zu hoch angegeben worden. Da waren die gefälschten Angaben aber schon in aller Welt. Um die Frage endgültig zu klären, wurde anlässlich des 800-jährigen Stadtjubiläums 2006 eine Historikerkommission eingesetzt. Ergebnis: maximal 25 000 Tote. Tragisch genug. ——— Die vermeintliche Einzigartigkeit der Zerstörung Dresdens wird durch zahlreiche populäre Werke gestützt. So bezog sich beispielsweise Kurt Vonnegut auf das Buch *Der Untergang von Dresden*, mit dem der spätere Holocaustleugner David Irving Geschichtsklitterung betrieben hatte. Martin Walser berichtet in *Die Verteidigung der Kindheit* von einem aus dem zerstörten Zirkus Sarrasani entlaufenen Löwen, der nicht etwa auf die Jagd geht, sondern sich, angesichts des Ausmaßes der Katastrophe, an die Überlebenden schmiegt.[21] Und Harry Mulisch hob die Stadt gleich gänzlich aus Zeit und Raum: „Etwas fehlte, man schrieb nicht das Jahr 1945, man war außerhalb der Geschichte, hunderttausend Jahre vor Christus. Erstaunlicher, als wenn ein Dinosaurier eines Tages sein Nest auf dem Innenhof des Zwingers gebaut hätte, war die Tatsache, daß niemand ein solches Tier in der Stadt entdeckt hat."[22] ——— Sehr konkret bemerkbar machten sich nach der deutschen Wiedervereinigung Rechtsextremisten, die den 13. Februar regelmäßig für sich in Anspruch nahmen. Auf ihren „Trauermärschen" war von einem „alliierten Bombenholocaust" die Rede – mit 500 000 Opfern. Auf dem Höhepunkt zogen 2005 6500 Neonazis durch Dresden. Gegen die Vereinnahmung formierte sich in den Folgejahren ein breiter Protest, dem es mitunter gelang, die Demonstrationsstrecke zu blockieren. Dresden wurde somit nicht nur zum Streitpunkt in Debatten um den richtigen Umgang mit zerstörter Architektur, es rückte zugleich auch in den Mittelpunkt der Auseinandersetzungen um ein angemessenes Gedenken an die deutschen Opfer des Zweiten Weltkriegs. ——— Ist es Zufall, dass sich die sich dauerhaft von Einwanderung bedroht fühlenden „patrio-

relativise Germany's guilt and to underscore its status as a victim of the war. Thus, Dresden and not the Battle of Britain, which had been instigated by the Germans, became the symbol for the destructive force of bombing campaigns. ——— The undoubtedly traumatising events of Dresden's bombing facilitated the creation of this myth. Eye witnesses (including, as we have seen, Victor Klemperer) reported of phosphorus bombs and of low-flying bombers taking aim at those fleeing across fields. Despite the fact that evidence for such claims was never provided, accounts of the alleged atrocities committed by Allied forces were widely propagated. The situation was not very different in the German Democratic Republic. Although German war crimes were now also acknowledged, the attacks on Dresden were invoked during the Cold War as an argument against imperialism. ——— How many people died in Dresden? The popularisation of inaccurate casualty figures is just one example of the biased treatment of facts and data. In 1966, for instance, their manipulation by fascist leaders was already revealed in a document that had been discovered at the federal archives in Koblenz. The reported numbers of persons killed or injured were too high by a factor of ten. By this time, however, the falsified data had already been disseminated worldwide. In 2006, which marked the city's 800th year, a committee of historians was appointed in order to resolve the question once and for all. The result: though certainly still tragic, there were at most 25,000 deaths. ——— The supposedly singular nature of Dresden's destruction is asserted in a number of popular works. Kurt Vonnegut, for instance, referenced *The Destruction of Dresden*, a book in which the Holocaust denier David Irving distorted history. In his novel *Die Verteidigung der Kindheit* (Defending Childhood), Martin Walser describes a lion that escapes from the destroyed Sarrasani Circus and, in the face of the catastrophic devastation, nestles up to survivors rather than going on the hunt.[21] And Harry Mulisch lifted the city out of time and space altogether: 'Something was missing. The year was not 1945; we were outside of history, one-hundred thousand years before

Historische Kutsche auf Zeitreise: der rekonstruierte Neumarkt im Jahr 2016. —— **Historical coach on a journey through time: the reconstructed Neumarkt square in 2016.**

tischen Europäer" der fremdenfeindlichen Bewegung PEGIDA um 2014/15 gerade in Sachsen formierten, in der Stadt, die so oft als Opfer der Geschichte dargestellt wurde? „Man muss nicht hier aufgewachsen sein, um zu begreifen, was diese Stadt zum Sonderfall macht", hatte Durs Grünbein bereits 1995 über den „Mythos Dresden" geschrieben. „Prachtvoll waren viele, einen tragischen Untergang hatten andere auch, aber keine kultivierte die Erinnerung an die Zeit vor der Zerstörung mit soviel [sic!] schmerzvoller Nostalgie, keine lebte so sehr vom Phantombild ihrer einstigen weltstädtischen Silhouette. Es war die Chimäre des Alten Dresdens, die überall umging, wie das Heimweh nach einer besseren Zeit."[23] —— Wenngleich Fritz Löffler seine historische Betrachtung im Februar 1945 enden ließ, blickte er hoffnungsvoll in die Zukunft: „So stehen wir heute am Beginn einer weiteren Epoche Dresdens", beschließt er das vorangestellte Memento, „von der wir hoffen, daß sie ruhmvoll ihre ganz neuen Aufgaben lösen und damit die große Tradition fortführen wird."[24] Mit *Dresden in drei Zeiten* wollen wir sehen, was die „weitere Epoche" der Stadt bislang gebracht hat, wie mit der Vergangenheit umgegangen und neue Herausforderungen angegangen wurden. Ge-

Christ. More astonishing than if a dinosaur had one day built its nest in the inner courtyard of the Zwinger Palace was the fact that nobody had discovered such an animal within the city.'[22] —— After the reunification of Germany, right-wing extremists specifically drew attention to themselves by regularly claiming the 13th of February for their own purposes. On their 'funeral marches', they spoke of an 'Allied bombing holocaust' with 500,000 victims. These events reached their height in 2005, when 6500 neo-Nazis demonstrated in the streets of Dresden. In the years that followed, this appropriation of history led to widespread protests, which were able to block the demonstration route at times. Dresden thus not only became an issue of contention in debates concerning the correct approach to dealing with destroyed architecture, it also moved to the centre of arguments about how to appropriately commemorate the German victims of the Second World War. —— Is it a coincidence that PEGIDA, the xenophobic movement of 'patriotic Europeans' who constantly feel threatened by immigrants, formed in Saxony and specifically in the city that has so often been portrayed as the victim of history? 'You do not need to have grown up here to understand what makes this city such a special case', Durs Grünbein had written about the 'Myth of Dresden' in 1995: 'There were many other magnificent cities, and others had also experienced a tragic demise, but no other city cultivated the memory of the time before its destruction with so much painful nostalgia. No other city relied to such an extent on the phantom image of its former cosmopolitan silhouette. It was the chimera of Old Dresden that circulated everywhere, like a longing for a better time.'[23] —— Though Fritz Löffler's historical survey ends in February 1945, he looks to the future with optimism. He closes his remembrance by stating, 'Today, Dresden stands at the dawn of another era, one we hope will solve its entirely new problems in a manner worthy of praise, thereby continuing the city's great tradition.'[24] In *Dresden in Three Eras*, we will examine what this further era has meant for the city so far, how it has dealt with the past and approached new challenges.

zeig werden 25 Dresdner Orte in drei verschiedenen Zeiten, die die geschichtlichen Kontinuitäten und Brüche sichtbar werden lassen.

1 Johann Gottfried Herder: „Kunstsammlungen in Dresden". In: ders. (Hg.): *Adrastea*, Bd. 3, Leipzig 1802, S. 56.

2 „100 Dresdner des 20. Jahrhunderts". In: *Dresdner Neueste Nachrichten*, 31.12.1999.

3 Hermann Rudolph: „Hüter des Mythos Dresden". In: *Die Zeit*, Nr. 8/1985, 15.2.1985.

4 Fritz Löffler: *Das alte Dresden*, Leipzig 2012, S. 8.

5 Ingo Schulze: „Ich war ein begeisterter Dresdner. Zum Auftakt der 800-Jahr Feier der sächsischen Hauptstadt – Nachtgedanken eines aus dem Ort Gefallenen". In: *Süddeutsche Zeitung*, 76/2006, 31.3.2006.

6 Johann Gottfried Herder: „Kunstsammlungen in Dresden". In: ders. (Hg.): *Adrastea*, Bd. 3, Leipzig 1802, S. 53.

7 Johann Wolfgang von Goethe: *Goethes Werke*, Bd. 9, München 2002, S. 324.

8 E. T. A. Hoffmann: *Der goldene Topf*, Berlin 2016, S. 3

9 Victor Klemperer: *LTI. Notizbuch eines Philologen*, Berlin 1947, S. 276.

10 Ders.: *Tagebücher 1935–1936*, Berlin 1999, S. 42.

11 Erich Kästner: *Werke*, Bd. 1, München 1998, S. 370.

12 Kurt Vonnegut: *Schlachthof 5 oder Der Kinderkreuzzug*, Reinbek bei Hamburg 1972, S. 172.

13 Otto Griebel: *Ich war ein Mann der Straße. Lebenserinnerungen eines Dresdner Malers*, Leipzig 1986. S. 428.

14 Victor Klemperer: *LTI. Notizbuch eines Philologen*, Berlin 1947, S. 393.

15 Aleida Montijn: *Nachrichten an K. G. Erinnerungen einer Komponistin*, Kassel 1998. Zit. n.: Walter Kempowski: *Der rote Hahn. Dresden im Februar 1945*, München 2001, S. 180.

16 Kurt Vonnegut: *Schlachthof 5 oder Der Kinderkreuzzug*, Reinbek bei Hamburg 1972, S. 173.

17 Ingo Schulze: „Ich war ein begeisterter Dresdner. Zum Auftakt der 800-Jahr Feier der sächsischen Hauptstadt – Nachtgedanken eines aus dem Ort Gefallenen." In: *Süddeutsche Zeitung*, 76/2006, 31.3.2006.

18 Helmut Kohl: *Erinnerungen. 1982–1990*, München 2005, S. 1025.

19 Thomas Rosenlöcher: *Die verkauften Pflastersteine. Dresdner Tagebuch*, Frankfurt a. M. 1990, S. 82.

20 Manfred Altner: *Gerhart Hauptmann in Dresden und Radebeul*, Dresden 2003, S. 89.

21 Vgl. Martin Walser: *Die Verteidigung der Kindheit*, Frankfurt a. M. 1997, S. 27.

22 Harry Mulisch: *Das steinerne Brautbett*, Hamburg 1960, S. 92.

23 Durs Grünbein: *Galilei vermißt Dantes Hölle und bleibt an den Maßen hängen. Aufsätze 1989–1995*, Frankfurt a. M. 1996, S. 151.

24 Fritz Löffler: *Das alte Dresden*, Leipzig 2012, S. 10.

Twenty-five sites in Dresden are shown from three different historical perspectives that reveal the continuities and ruptures in the city's history.

1 Johann Gottfried Herder, 'Kunstsammlungen in Dresden', in *Adrastea* (Leipzig: 1802), III, p. 56. Unless otherwise noted, all quotations have been translated into English by Kristine Jennings.

2 '100 Dresdner des 20. Jahrhunderts', n *Dresdner Neueste Nachrichten*, 31 December 1999.

3 Hermann Rudolph, 'Hüter des Mythos Dresden', in *Die Zeit*, 15 February 1985 (8).

4 Fritz Löffler, *Das alte Dresden* (Leipzig: 2012), p. 8.

5 Ingo Schulze, 'Ich war ein begeisterter Dresdner. Zum Auftakt der 800-Jahr Feier der sächsischen Hauptstadt – Nachtgedanken eines aus dem Ort Gefallenen', in *Süddeutsche Zeitung*, 31 March 2006 (76).

6 Johann Gottfied Herder, 'Kunstsammlungen in Dresden', see note 1, p. 53.

7 Johann Wolfgang von Goethe, *Truth and Fiction Relating to My Life*, trans. by John Oxenford, in *The Works of J. W. von Goethe*, ed. by Nathan Haskell Dole (New York: 1902), II, pp. 350–51.

8 E. T. A. Hoffmann, *The Golden Flower Pot* (Berkshire: 2008), p. 1.

9 Victor Klemperer, *LTI. Notizbuch eines Philologen* (Berlin: 1947), p. 276.

10 Victor Klemperer, Tagebücher 1935–1936 (Berlin: 1999), p. 42.

11 Erich Kästner, *Werke* (Munich: 1998), I, p. 370.

12 Kurt Vonnegut, Jr., *Slaughterhouse-Five, Or the Children's Crusade: A Duty-dance with Death* (St Albans: 1972) <https://archive.org/details/SlaughterhouseFiveOrTheChildrensCrusade/page/n79> [accessed 13 February 2019].

13 Otto Griebel, *Ich war ein Mann der Strasse. Lebenserinnerungen eines Dresdner Malers* (Leipzig: 1986), p. 428.

14 Victor Klemperer, *LTI. Notizbuch eines Philologen*, see note 9, p. 393.

15 Aleida Montijn, *Nachrichten an K. G. Erinnerungen einer Komponistin* (Kassel: 1998). Quoted in Walter Kempowski, *Der rote Hahn. Dresden im Februar 1945* (Munich: 2001), p. 180

16 Kurt Vonnegut, Jr., *Slaughterhouse-Five*, see note 12, p. 173.

17 Ingo Schulze, 'Ich war ein begeisterter Dresdner', see note 5.

18 Helmut Kohl, *Erinnerungen. 1982–1990* (Munich: 2005), p. 1025.

19 Thomas Rosenlöcher, *Die verkauften Pflastersteine. Dresdner Tagebuch* (Frankfurt: 1990), p. 82.

20 Manfred Altner, *Gerhart Hauptmann in Dresden und Radebeul* (Dresden: 2003), p. 89.

21 See Martin Walser, *Die Verteidigung der Kindheit* (Frankfurt: 1997), p. 27.

22 Harry Mulisch, *Das steinerne Brautbett* (Hamburg: 1960), p. 92.

23 Durs Grünbein, *Galilei vermisst Dantes Hölle und bleibt an den Maßen hängen. Aufsätze 1989–1995* (Frankfurt: 1996), p. 151.

24 Fritz Löffler, *Das alte Dresden* (Leipzig: 2012), p. 10.

WIENER PLATZ

„Merkwürdig bescheiden bleibt der Einfluß des Jugendstils auf die Dresdner Architektur", bilanziert Fritz Löffler in *Das alte Dresden*. „Eine Sonderstellung nahm Kurt Diestels Kaisercafé, der Eckbau Prager-/Wiener Platz am Hauptbahnhof ein."[1] Die Fassaden des 1902 errichteten Büro- und Geschäftshauses hatten deutlich Einflüsse der Wiener Secession gezeigt. Eigentlicher Eigentümer war die Dresdner Feuerversicherung, die ihre Geschäfte alsbald auf das gesamte Deutsche Reich ausdehnte. Aller Tüchtigkeit zum Trotz ging der Genossenschaftssitz im Februar 1945 in Flammen auf – das Kaisercafé hatte allerdings bereits Jahre zuvor geschlossen. Die Feuersozietät wurde von der Gothaer Versicherungsbank übernommen, ihr Stammsitz wie so viele andere Gebäude am Wiener Platz nicht neu errichtet. Heute wird er im Norden vom Prager Carrée mit dem Neuen Glaskugelhaus sowie der sogenannten „Prager Spitze" begrenzt – im Hinblick auf die modernen Glasfassaden nimmt sich der Einfluss des Jugendstils in beiden Fällen jedoch bescheiden aus.

1 Fritz Löffler: *Das alte Dresden*, Leipzig 2012, S. 416.

WIENER PLATZ

In *Das alte Dresden*, Fritz Löffler concludes that 'Art Nouveau's influence on the architecture of Dresden has been strangely restrained. Kurt Diestel's Kaisercafé, the corner building at the intersection of Prager Platz and Wiener Platz near the central railway station, holds a privileged position.'[1] Built in 1902, the facade of the office and shop building was clearly influenced by the Vienna Secession. The building was owned by the fire insurance company Dresdner Feuerversicherung, which was able to quickly expand its business operations to the entire German Reich. Despite the company's efficiency, its headquarters went up in flames in February 1945 (the Kaisercafé had already closed several years prior to this). Dresdner Feuerversicherung was subsumed by Gothaer Versicherungsbank, and its main office, like so many other buildings at Wiener Platz, was not rebuilt. Today, the square is bordered in the north by the Prager Carrée building complex, with the new Glaskugelhaus (a spherical glass structure), and the long, narrow building known as the 'Prager Spitze'. In light of the modern glass facades of both, it would appear that Art Nouveau has only had a moderate influence here.

1 Fritz Löffler, *Das alte Dresden* (Leipzig: 2012), p. 416.

Markanter Auftakt der Prager Straße: das auch als Kaisercafé bekannte Haus der Dresdner Feuerversicherung sowie das Prager Carrée mit dem Neuen Glaskugelhaus und die „Prager Spitze". ———
Prager Strasse's distinctive start: the building that housed the insurance company Dresdner Feuerversicherung (it was also known as the Kaisercafé) and the Prager Carrée with the new Glaskugelhaus and the 'Prager Spitze'.

PRAGER STRASSE

Als Erich Kästner nach dem Zweiten Weltkrieg seiner Heimatstadt einen Besuch abstattet, traut er seinen Augen kaum: „Ich stand auf der Prager Straße? Auf der weltberühmten Prager Straße? Auf der prächtigsten Straße meiner Kindheit? Auf der Straße mit den schönsten Schaufenstern? Auf der herrlichsten Straße der Weihnachtszeit? Ich stand in einer kilometerlangen, kilometerbreiten Leere", erinnert er sich im autobiografischen Roman *Als ich ein kleiner Junge war*. „In einer Ziegelsteppe. Im Garnichts."[2] Von der geschäftigen Korridorstraße, die Mitte des 19. Jahrhunderts entstanden war, ist kaum etwas geblieben. ——— Später fällt auch die letzte erhaltene Bausubstanz, die Hauptverkehrsachse vom Hauptbahnhof zum Altmarkt wird zu einem „gesellschaftlichen Erlebnisweg"[3], so der Generalbebauungsplan der Stadt Dresden aus dem Jahr 1967, transformiert. Die ursprüngliche Konzeption wurde bei den stadtplanerischen Eingriffen nach der Wiedervereinigung allerdings kaum berücksichtigt – und so sucht man auch die Flaniermeile im Sinne der sozialistischen Großstadt, eine der ersten deutschen Fußgängerzonen, heute vergeblich.

[2] Erich Kästner: *Als ich ein kleiner Junge war*, München 2003, S. 64.

[3] Rat der Stadt Dresden (Hg.): *Generalbebauungsplan und Generalverkehrsplan der Stadt Dresden*, Dresden 1967, S. 28.

PRAGER STRASSE

When Erich Kästner visited his home town after the Second World War, he could hardly believe his eyes. His impressions are captured in his autobiographical novel *Als ich ein kleiner Junge war* (When I Was a Little Boy): 'Was I really standing on Prager Strasse? On the world-famous Prager Strasse? On the most magnificent street I had seen as a child? On the street with the loveliest shop windows? On the most wonderful street of the Christmas season? I was standing in a barren space a mile long and a mile wide. On a steppe of bricks. In an absolute void.'[2] Almost nothing was left of the busy shop-lined street that had emerged in the nineteenth century. ——— Some time later, even the last remaining structure collapsed, and the main axis of traffic between the central railway station and the Altmarkt square was supposed to be transformed into a 'social experience trail', according to the 1967 general development plan for the city of Dresden.[3] However, the original concept was largely neglected in the urban development measures that were implemented after reunification, and the promenade that was envisioned for the socialist metropolis, one of the first German pedestrian areas, is nowhere to be seen today.

[2] Erich Kästner, *Als ich ein kleiner Junger war* (Munich: 2003), p. 64.

[3] Dresden City Council, *Generalbebauungsplan und Generalverkehrsplan der Stadt Dresden* (Dresden: 1967), p. 28.

1909

Stark frequentierte Geschäftsstraße, brachliegende Fläche, verkehrsberuhigter Erlebnisweg – die Prager Straße. —— Prager Strasse as high-traffic shopping street, barren land, and traffic-calmed social experience trail.

1958

2013

EHEMALIGES CENTRAL-THEATER

„Bald wurden die Dresdner Theater mein zweites Zuhause. Und oft mußte mein Vater allein zu Abend essen, weil Mama und ich, meist auf Stehplätzen, der Muse Thalia huldigten. Unser Abendbrot fand in der großen Pause statt. In Treppenwinkeln. Dort wurden die Wurstsemmeln ausgewickelt. Und das Butterbrotpapier verschwand, säuberlich gefaltet, wieder in Mutters brauner Handtasche."[4] Erich Kästner war, wie wir aus seinem Roman *Als ich ein kleiner Junge war* wissen, ein Liebhaber der darstellenden Künste. Albert-Theater, Schauspielhaus und Oper sind für den angehenden Schriftsteller am Beginn des 20. Jahrhunderts die Hotspots, fester Bestandteil der vielfältigen Kulturlandschaft seinerzeit war aber auch das Central-Theater in der Waisenhausstraße. Das privat geführte Haus war 1898 eröffnet worden und wartete mit einer neobarocken Fassade auf. Rasch stieg es zur bestimmenden Bühne des städtischen Operettenspiels auf – und so mancher Zuschauer mag sich nach der Vorstellung zu einer Brotzeit ins „Tunnel" genannte Bierrestaurant zurückgezogen haben, das bis zu 1000 Gäste aufnehmen konnte.

[4] Erich Kästner: *Als ich ein kleiner Junge war*, München 2003, S. 133 f.

FORMER CENTRAL THEATRE

'The theatres of Dresden soon became my second home. And Father often had to eat his dinner alone because Mama and I were paying homage to the muse Thalia, most often in standing places. We ate our evening meal during the intermission. In the corners of stairways, we unpacked our sausage rolls, and the sandwich paper disappeared again, neatly folded, in Mother's brown handbag.'[4] As revealed in his novel *Als ich ein kleiner Junge war*, Erich Kästner was a lover of the performing arts. The Albert Theatre, the *Schauspielhaus* (Playhouse), and the opera were the aspiring writer's hotspots at the beginning of the twentieth century. However, the Central Theatre on Waisenhausstrasse was also integral to the diverse cultural landscape of the time. The privately managed establishment was opened in 1898 and boasted a neo-Baroque facade. It quickly advanced to become the city's foremost stage for operetta, and it is likely that many a spectator retreated to the so-called 'Tunnel', a tavern that could seat up to one thousand guests, for a sandwich after the show.

[4] Erich Kästner, *Als ich ein kleiner Junge war*, pp. 133–34.

Die tragische Geschichte des ehemaligen Central-Theaters in der Waisenhausstraße sowie eine Hinterbühne der modernen Warenwelt. —— The tragic history of the former Central Theatre on Waisenhausstrasse and a backstage of the modern world of consumption.

NEUES RATHAUS

Die Frau hat die Arbeit, und der Mann grüßt fröhlich mit dem Füllhorn – ganz gendergerecht gibt sich das Neue Rathaus auf den ersten Blick nicht. Immerhin erinnert das Denkmal vor dem Festsaalflügel an die Helferinnen, die nach dem Zweiten Weltkrieg zur Enttrümmerung Dresdens beitrugen. Auch die südöstliche Altstadt musste von Schuttbergen beräumt werden, dabei war die jüngere Stätte der Stadtoberen, obschon das Alte Rathaus der Verwaltung längst zu klein geworden war, erst 1910 eingeweiht worden. ——— Doch selbst der Herkules auf der Spitze hat schwere Zeiten gesehen – so hielt er sich selbstredend auch während der Bombardierung Dresdens in luftiger Höhe auf. Am 14. Februar 1945 war der Turm ausgebrannt, die Zeiger der Uhr waren um halb drei in der Nacht stehen geblieben und der Goldene Rathausmann, der die rechte Hand zum Schutz über die Stadt erhebt, zeigte sich von Splittern durchlöchert. Die Rekonstruktion des Verwaltungssitzes wurde erst 1965 mit dem Neuaufbau des abgebildeten Festsaalflügels abgeschlossen.

NEW TOWN HALL A woman at work and a friendly greeting from a man with a cornucopia—at first glance, the New Town Hall doesn't make a gender-equitable impression. However, the monument in front of the ballroom wing reminds one of the women who helped to clear the city's wreckage after the Second World War. Mountains of rubble also needed to be removed from the historic centre in the south-eastern district of the city, where the new site of municipal administration had only been inaugurated in 1910 (despite the fact that the Old Town Hall had long been outgrown). ——— Even the Hercules sitting atop the building's clock tower has witnessed hard times since, naturally, he retained his lofty position even during the bombing of Dresden. On 14 February 1945, the tower was burnt out, the hands of the clock stopped at half past two in the morning, and the golden figure, with his right hand raised to shield the city, was punctured by splinters. The reconstruction of the administrative centre was not completed until 1965, when construction ended on the ballroom wing (seen in the images on the opposite page).

Das Neue Rathaus mit und ohne Trümmerfrau. —— The New Town Hall with and without woman clearing rubble (the so-called 'Trümmerfrau').

DIONYSOS VOR DEM RATSKELLER

„Trink ihn aus, den Trank der Labe", heißt es in Friedrich Schillers Gedicht *Das Siegesfest*, „Und vergiß den großen Schmerz, // Wundervoll ist Bacchus' Gabe, // Balsam fürs zerrißne Herz!"[5] An der Elbe hatte der Dichter Erfahrungen mit der Rebe sammeln können, schließlich bewohnte er von 1785 bis 1787 zeitweise ein auf einem Weinberg gelegenes Gartenhäuschen seines Förderers Christian Gottfried Körner in Loschwitz. ——— Der zweitbekannteste Weinkenner der Stadt ist Georg Wrba, 1910 postierte der Bildhauer *Bacchus auf einem trunkenen Esel reitend* vor dem Neuen Rathaus. Die Bronzeskulptur gilt nicht nur als eines der populärsten, sondern auch als eines der volksnahsten Bildwerke Dresdens – schließlich soll es Glück bringen, den großen Zeh des Reiters zu berühren. Fortuna war Dionysos, so die eigentliche Bezeichnung für den Gott des Weines, auch im Februar 1945 hold. In seiner Autobiografie *Ich war ein Mann der Straße* erinnert sich der Maler Otto Griebel auch an das verwüstete Verwaltungsgebäude seiner Heimatstadt: „Nur der ‚Rathausesel' mit seinem trunkenen Reiter stand noch wie ehedem am Eingange des Ratskellers, schier wie ein Hohn auf all die Zerstörung ringsum."[6]

[5] Georg Kurscheidt (Hg.): *Schiller. Werke und Briefe in zwölf Bänden. Band 1: Gedichte*, Frankfurt a. M. 1992, S. 343–347.

[6] Otto Griebel: *Ich war ein Mann der Straße. Lebenserinnerungen eines Dresdner Malers*, Leipzig 1986, S. 461.

DIONYSUS IN FRONT OF THE RATSKELLER

'Drink of this: it will restore, | And forget thy grievous smart; | Wonderful is Bacchus' power | To relieve a tortured heart', Friedrich Schiller writes in his poem 'Das Siegesfest' (translated as 'The Feast of Victory').[5] The poet had become acquainted with the grapevine during his time at the Elbe River; between 1785 and 1787, he occasionally resided in Loschwitz, in a vineyard cottage belonging to his patron Christian Gottfried Körner. ——— After Schiller, the city's most famous wine lover is Georg Wrba, the sculptor who, in 1910, placed 'Bacchus Riding on a Drunken Donkey' before the New Town Hall. The unpretentious bronze statue is one of the most popular sculptures in Dresden, and touching the rider's large toe is said to bring good luck. Dionysus, as the god of wine was originally called by the Greeks, was also favoured by the goddess Fortuna in February 1945. In his autobiography, *Ich war ein Mann der Strasse* [I Was a Man of the Streets], the painter Otto Griebel remembers the ruin that remained of his city's administrative building: 'Only the "Town Hall donkey" and his drunken rider still stood at the entrance to the Ratskeller [the Town Hall's basement restaurant], as if to mock the destruction all around.'[6]

[5] Friedrich Schiller, 'The Feast of Victory', in *The Poems of Schiller*, trans. by E.P. Arnold-Forster (London: 1901), p. 140.

[6] Otto Griebel, *Ich war ein Mann der Strasse. Lebenserinnerungen eines Dresdner Malers* (Leipzig: 1986), p. 461.

Zerrissenes Herz und zerstörte Stadt: die Skulptur *Bacchus auf einem trunkenen Esel reitend* vor dem Ratskeller. —— A 'tortured heart' and a city in ruins: the statue of *Bacchus Riding on a Drunken Donkey* in front of the Ratskeller.

ALTMARKT
MIT KREUZKIRCHE

„Die Vergangenheit ist mit Recht ein Spiegel der Zukunft zu nennen, und deswegen ist schon zum bessern Verständniß der Zeitgeschichte die Kenntniß der alten Welt nützlich"[7], heißt es in der Einleitung des Verfassers in der *Denkwürdigen Geschichtschronik der Schildbürger* – doch am Altmarkt, an dem der Dichter Ludwig Tieck von 1819 bis 1841 lebte, sucht man vergeblich nach Reflexionen alter Zeiten. Von den prächtigen Häusern der Renaissance, die einst den Platz säumten, hielt keins den Angriffen aus der Luft stand. ——— Geblieben ist lediglich ein Gotteshaus, das zuvor bereits mehrmals zerstört worden war. Der ursprüngliche Sakralbau war noch St. Nikolai gewidmet, dann aber brachte Constanze von Österreich anlässlich ihrer Heirat mit dem Markgrafen Heinrich von Meißen eine Kreuzreliquie nach Dresden, die in einer nahe stehenden Kapelle aufbewahrt wurde. Über die Jahre übertrug sich der Name auf die Kirche. ——— Am Fuße der Kreuzkirche findet seit 1434 der Striezelmarkt statt, er zählt damit zu den ältesten Weihnachtsmärkten der Welt. Die winterliche Tradition hat sich durch alle Zeiten erhalten und ist damit ein lebendiger Spiegel der Vergangenheit.

7 Ludwig Tieck: *Schriften*, Band 9, Berlin 1828, S. 4.

ALTMARKT SQUARE WITH THE CHURCH OF THE HOLY CROSS

'The past is rightly called the mirror of the future, and, therefore, if we wish to have a better understanding of contemporary history, it would be useful to have some knowledge of the old world', Ludwig Tieck asserts in the introduction to *Denkwürdige Geschichtschronik der Schildbürger* [The Memorable History of the Burghers of Schilda].[7] However, at Altmarkt square, where the writer lived from 1819 to 1841, reflections of the past are nowhere to be found. Not one of the splendid Renaissance buildings that once stood here survived the aerial attacks of the Second World War. ——— The only structure that remained was a church that had been destroyed on multiple occasions before this. The original ecclesiastical building had been dedicated to St Nicholas. However, a True Cross relic was brought to Dresden by Constance of Austria after her marriage to Henry III, Margrave of Meissen. It was housed in a nearby chapel, and over the years, the church became known by the same name. ——— The *Striezelmarkt* has been taking place at the foot of the Church of the Holy Cross since 1434 and is thus one of the oldest Christmas markets worldwide. This winter tradition, which has been preserved throughout the city's history, is a living mirror of the past.

7 Ludwig Tieck, *Schriften* (Berlin: 1828), IX, p. 4.

Die alte und die neue Welt: der Altmarkt samt Kreuz-kirche. —— The old world and the new: Altmarkt square and the Church of the Holy Cross.

LUTHER-DENKMAL

1883 ergeht im Dresdner Anzeiger der Aufruf, für ein Standbild auf dem Neumarkt zu spenden: „Laßt sein erhabenes Bild in der Kraft und Schönheit, wie es einst Meister Rietschels Hand hier geschaffen, in Erz uns gießen und auf einem öffentlichen Platze unserer Stadt auch zu deren Ehre aufrichten. Zu diesem Zwecke sind wir zusammengetreten. Jede, auch die kleinste Gabe soll uns willkommen sein als Zeugniß für Dr. Martin Luther."[8] Ernst Rietschel hatte bereits dem Luther-Denkmal in Worms die Form gegeben, ein damals nicht verwendetes Modell des Kopfes soll nun, anlässlich des 400. Jahrestags von Luthers Geburt, zum Einsatz kommen. ——— Als Distriktsvikar hatte Luther Dresden 1516 sowie 1518 einen Besuch abgestattet, der sächsische Kurfürst Friedrich der Weise sollte zum Schutzherrn des aufbegehrenden Kirchenmanns werden. Weniger Glück war dem Abbild des Reformators beschieden, die Bomben des Zweiten Weltkriegs schmetterten das ihm zu Ehren geschaffene Denkmal zu Boden, von 1955 an hatte Luther ein halbes Jahrhundert die Ruine der Frauenkirche im Rücken.

[8] Erste Beilage zum *Dresdner Anzeiger*, 304/1883, 31. Oktober 1883.

MARTIN LUTHER MONUMENT

In 1883, Dresden's newspaper, the *Dresdner Anzeiger*, called for donations for a statue at Neumarkt square: 'Let us cast his noble image in bronze, with the same strength and beauty once created here by Master Rietschel's hand, and let us erect this figure in his honour in a public square of our city. We have assembled for this purpose. We welcome even the smallest contribution as a tribute to Dr Martin Luther.'[8] Ernst Rietschel had already designed the Luther monument in Worms, and a model of the head that had not been used at the time was now to become part of the monument in honour of the 400th anniversary of Luther's birth. ——— As the district curate, Luther had visited Dresden in 1516 and 1518. Frederick III, Elector of Saxony (also known as Frederick the Wise), would become the aspiring ecclesiastic's patron. The reformer's likeness was less fortunate, however, as the monument created in Luther's honour was shattered by bombs during the Second World War. Re-erected in 1955, Luther would stand before the ruins of the Church of our Lady for half a century.

[8] First supplement in the *Dresdner Anzeiger*, 31 October 304/1883.

Bild der Erhabenheit, Zeugnis der Zerstörung: das Denkmal für „Deutschlands größten Sohn"[9] vor der Frauenkirche. —— An image of grandeur, proof of destruction: the monument to 'Germany's greatest son'[9] in front of the Church of Our Lady.

9 Ebd. — Ibid.

FRAUENKIRCHE

Der Archivar Otto Richter hat sich derart um die Aufzeichnung des Stadtgeschehens verdient gemacht, dass man ihn den „Vater der Geschichte Dresdens" nennt. Über die architektonische Hinterlassenschaft Augusts des Starken bemerkte er u.a.: „Schliesslich wurde unter Augusts förderndem Einfluss auch noch das gewaltige Bauwerk begonnen, das mit seiner majestätischen Kuppel dem Stadtbilde für alle Zeiten seine schönsten Linien gegeben hat: die Frauenkirche."[10] George Bährs Entwurf eines barocken Sakralbaus war 1743 vollendet worden und hatte sich nicht nur für den Neumarkt, sondern für das gesamte Stadtpanaroma zum bestimmenden Element entwickelt. ——— Im Zuge der Luftangriffe brannte die Kirche vollständig aus, letztlich hielten die Stützpfeiler der Last des Gewölbes nicht mehr stand. Zu DDR-Zeiten wurden die Trümmer als Mahnmal bewahrt. Die Kosten des Wiederaufbaus, alsbald nach der Wende begonnen, wurden überwiegend von privaten Spendern getragen. Anlässlich der Eröffnung am 30. Oktober 2005 nannte der damalige Bundespräsident, Horst Köhler, die neue Frauenkirche ein Symbol der Versöhnung.

[10] Otto Richter: *Canaletto-Mappe*, Dresden 1895, S. 3.

THE CHURCH OF OUR LADY

The important work performed by the archivist Otto Richter in chronicling the city's past earned him the title 'Father of Dresden's History'. With regard to the architectural legacy of Augustus the Strong, he noted, 'The Church of Our Lady, the colossal structure whose majestic cupola has forever given the city its most beautiful contours, was also begun under Augustus's patronage.'[10] The Baroque church, designed by George Bähr, was completed in 1743 and became a defining element of Neumarkt square and of the entire city skyline. ——— During the course of the air strikes on the city, the church was completely burnt out and, finally, its pillars were no longer able to support the weight of the structure. In the GDR era, the ruins were preserved as a memorial. The church's restoration, begun soon after Germany's reunification, was largely paid for by private donations. At the inauguration on 30 October 2005, Horst Köhler, Germany's Federal President at the time, called the new Church of our Lady a symbol of reconciliation.

[10] Otto Richter, *Canaletto-Mappe* (Dresden: 1895), p. 3.

ca. 1897

2013

1945

Mahnmal gegen den Krieg, Symbol der Versöhnung: die Dresdner Frauenkirche. —— Reminder of the war and symbol of reconciliation: Dresden's Church of Our Lady.

MÜNZGASSE

„Eine Gruppe Leute kletterte die Anlagen hinauf zur Brühlterrasse. Ich stand dann oben, im Sturmwind und Funkenregen. Rechts und links flammten Gebäude, das Belvedere und – wahrscheinlich – die Kunstakademie [...]. Im weiteren Umkreis nichts als Brände."[11] ——— Die Elbterrasse, auf der Victor Klemperer während der Luftangriffe auf Dresden Schutz suchte, diente zunächst als Befestigungsanlage, wurde aber beginnend 1739 unter der Ägide des einflussreichen sächsischen Ministers Heinrich von Brühl im Stil des Dresdner Rokoko bebaut. Von den „Brühlschen Herrlichkeiten" ist nur der Garten geblieben, aber auch die nachfolgenden Bauten gaben sich ansehnlich – im 19. Jahrhundert war vom „Balkon Europas" die Rede. ——— Zum Neumarkt gewandt sprach man hingegen vom „Malerblick". Nach dem Zweiten Weltkrieg blieb die Münzgasse lange Zeit Brache, erst 1987 wurden wieder Gebäude errichtet, zum Teil in Plattenbauweise mit historisierender Fassade. Heute nimmt sie sich allerdings etwas weniger harmonisch aus – die Lage zwischen Frauenkirche und Terrassenufer hat sie zur stark frequentierten Gastrostrecke werden lassen.

[11] Victor Klemperer: *Tagebücher 1945*, Berlin 1999, S. 34.

MÜNZGASSE

'A group of people were clambering up through the public gardens to the Brühl Terrace.' [...] Then I was standing at the top in the storm wind and the showers of sparks. To right and left buildings were ablaze, the Belvedere—probably the Art Academy. [...] Within a wider radius nothing but fires.'[11] ——— The terrace on the Elbe River where Victor Klemperer sought shelter during the air raids was initially used as a fortification, but as of 1739, under the aegis of Saxony's influential prime minister Heinrich von Brühl, it was redesigned in the style of Dresden's Rococo. Only the garden remains of what was once known as 'Brühl's Glories', but the other structures built on Brühl Terrace were also impressive; in the nineteenth century, the terrace was referred to as 'the balcony of Europe'. ——— The view of the street leading from here to Neumarkt square likewise had its charms and was described as a 'painter's scene'. For a long time after the Second World War, the alley known as Münzgasse remained a wasteland. New buildings were not constructed until 1987. A portion of these were prefabricated buildings with historicising facades (so-called 'Plattenbauten'), but, today, the street has a less harmonious effect. Situated between the Church of Our Lady and Brühl Terrace, it has become a much-frequented area offering a variety of culinary options.

[11] Victor Klemperer, *To the Bitter End. The Diaries of Victor Klemperer*, trans. by Martin Chalmers (London: 1999), p. 391.

Malerisch bis historisierend: die Münzgasse, von der Brühlschen Terrasse aus betrachtet. —
From picturesque to historicising: Münzgasse as seen from Brühl's Terrace.

RESIDENZSCHLOSS

Von der mittelalterlichen Burg bis zur modernen Rekonstruktion gewährt das Residenzschloss einen Blick auf fast 800 Jahre sächsische Geschichte. Hatten ab Mitte des 15. Jahrhunderts die jeweiligen Landesherren ihren Wohnsitz im Schloss, residieren heute die Staatlichen Kunstsammlungen Dresden am Theaterplatz. Grünes Gewölbe, Türckische Cammer, der Riesensaal der Rüstkammer, Münzkabinett und Kupferstichkabinett unter einem Dach – daran war nach dem Zweiten Weltkrieg lange nicht zu denken. Erst 1985 wurde mit dem Wiederaufbau begonnen. In seiner Biografie berichtete Ernst Heinrich Prinz von Sachsen, jüngster Sohn des letzten sächsischen Königs, Friedrich August III., was das Bombardement aus dem ältesten Gebäude der Stadt gemacht hatte: „Nach Verlassen der Hofkirche sah ich mir das Residenzschloß an, in dem ich von 1904 bis 1914 meine Jugend verbracht hatte. Der Anblick war erschütternd. Ausgebrannt und verstümmelt stand dieser so schöne deutsche Renaissancebau da. Und auch sonst, wohin ich blickte – nichts als Trümmer."[12]

12 Ernst Heinrich Prinz von Sachsen: *Mein Lebensweg vom Königsschloß zum Bauernhof*, Dresden 1995, S. 289.

THE ROYAL PALACE

From the medieval castle to its modern reconstruction, the Royal Palace offers a glimpse into nearly eight hundred years of Saxony's history. As of the mid-fifteenth century, the palace served as the residence for the region's sovereigns; today, however, the Dresden State Art Collections are housed here at Theaterplatz. The Green Vault, the Turkish Chamber, the gigantic Armoury, the Coin Cabinet, and the Cabinet of Prints, Drawings, and Photographs are all located under one roof—a concept that was inconceivable for many years following the Second World War. The palace's reconstruction was not begun until 1985. In his biography, Prince Ernst Heinrich of Saxony, the youngest son of the last Saxon monarch, Frederick Augustus III, reports on the state of the city's oldest building after the bombing: 'After leaving the court church, I gazed upon the Royal Palace where I had spent my youth from 1904 to 1914. The sight was devastating. The beautiful German Renaissance building stood before me scorched and mutilated. And everywhere I looked—nothing but ruins.'[12]

12 Prince Ernst Heinrich of Saxony, *Mein Lebensweg vom Königsschloss zum Bauernhof* (Dresden: 1995), p. 289.

Eines der ältesten Gebäude der Stadt: das Residenzschloss mit der „Schinkelwache" im Vordergrund. —— One of the city's oldest buildings: the Royal Palace with the 'Schinkelwache' (the guard post named after Karl Friedrich Schinkel) in the foreground.

BLICK VOM GEORGENTOR

Der Wiederaufbau der Frauenkirche wurde von vielen Geschichten begleitet, besonders symbolisch aber ist die Entstehung des Kreuzes, das heute auf der Spitze zu sehen ist. Ursprünglich hatte dort das sogenannte Kuppelkreuz seinen Platz gehabt. Das von Johann George Schmidt, einem Cousin George Bährs, hergestellte Original war zwar 1993 in den Trümmern der Kirche entdeckt worden, allerdings so schwer beschädigt, dass es ersetzt werden musste. ——— „Bis zu zehn Stunden am Tag verbrachte ich bei großer Hitze in meiner Werkstatt, acht Monate lang“, berichtete Alan Smith dem *Cicero*. „Den Stahl und das Kupfer des Kreuzes hämmerte ich nach den alten Schmiedetechniken des 18. Jahrhunderts.“[13] Smith ist nicht irgendein Kunstschmied aus London – er ist auch der Sohn eines Piloten der Royal Air Force, der 1945 Bomben über der Stadt abwarf. Finanziert wird Smiths Arbeit u. a. vom britischen Dresden Trust. Das „sieben Meter hohe vergoldete Kreuz aus Stahl ist die Krönung meiner Laufbahn“, fährt er im Artikel fort. „Es war wie die Fertigung eines sehr komplizierten Puzzles, in dem sich die Vergangenheit und die Zukunft nahtlos ineinander fügen.“

[13] Alan Smith: „Auferstanden aus Ruinen“. In: *Cicero – Magazin für politische Kultur*, Berlin 2004, S. 124.

VIEW FROM GEORGE'S GATE The reconstruction of the Church of Our Lady was the subject of many anecdotes, but the cross that sits atop the church today has a particularly symbolic story. The original cupola cross, created by Johann George Schmidt, George Bähr's cousin, was discovered among the church ruins in 1993, but was so severely damaged that it had to be replaced. ——— 'For eight long months, I spent up to ten hours a day in my sweltering workshop', Alan Smith told the magazine *Cicero*. 'I hammered the steel and copper according to old forging techniques of the eighteenth century.'[13] Not just any artist blacksmith from London, Smith is also the son of a Royal Air Force pilot who dropped bombs on Dresden in 1945. Smith's work was financed by the British Dresden Trust, among others. In the *Cicero* article mentioned above, he declares that the 'seven-metre high gold-plated cross of steel is the crowning achievement of my career. It was like assembling a very complicated puzzle in which the past and the future are seamlessly intertwined.'

[13] Alan Smith, 'Auferstanden aus Ruinen', in *Cicero – Magazin für politische Kultur* (Berlin: 2004), p. 124.

Vom Kuppel- zum Versöhnungskreuz: die Altstadt mitsamt der Frauenkirche vom Georgentor aus betrachtet. —— From the cupola cross to the cross of reconciliation: the historic centre with the Church of Our Lady as seen from George's Gate.

BLICK VOM HAUSMANNSTURM

„Plötzlich blickte ich dankbar auf den Kulturpalast und auf die Rückfront des klobigen, unschönen Häuserriegels der früheren Thälmannstraße, nun wieder Wilsdruffer Straße, weil aus ihnen noch ein historisch fassbarer Bezug, eine konkrete Zeit sprach."[14] Ingo Schulzes Empfindungen beim Anblick sozialistischer Architektur, die er in seinem Essay *Ich war ein begeisterter Dresdner* niederschrieb, kann längst nicht jeder nachvollziehen. Heftig umstritten war beispielsweise der Kulturpalast, ein modernistischer Kubus, der bis 1969 am Altmarkt errichtet worden war und beim Blick vom Hausmannsturm den Abschnitt zwischen Residenzschloss und Kreuzkirche dominiert. Nach der Wiedervereinigung stand zwischenzeitlich gar ein vollständiger Abriss im Raum. Eine Bürgerinitiative setzte sich für den Erhalt ein. 2017 wurde ein mehrjähriger Umbau abgeschlossen, aus dem Mehrzwecksaal ist ein Orpheum für die Dresdner Philharmoniker geworden. Und der Solitär an der Wilsdruffer Straße gibt weiterhin einen augenfälligen Bezug zur Vergangenheit.

14 Ingo Schulze: „Ich war ein begeisterter Dresdner. Zum Auftakt der 800-Jahr Feier der sächsischen Hauptstadt – Nachtgedanken eines aus dem Ort Gefallenen". In: *Süddeutsche Zeitung*, 76/2006, 31.3.2006.

VIEW FROM THE HAUSMANN TOWER

'Suddenly, I felt thankful as I looked at the Palace of Culture and at the back of the ugly, hulking row of houses on what had once been Thälmannstrasse, now Wilsdruffer Strasse once more, because they embodied a tangible historic reference and spoke of a specific era.'[14] Ingo Schulze's sentiments at the sight of socialist architecture, as recorded in his essay 'Ich war ein begeisterter Dresdner', are certainly not shared by everyone. The Palace of Culture, for instance, was deeply controversial; the modernist cube was completed at Altmarkt square in 1969, and it dominates the view of the area between the Royal Palace and the Church of the Holy Cross as seen from the Hausmann Tower. After Germany's reunification, the city even considered demolishing the building, but a citizens' initiative campaigned to preserve it. Several years of construction were concluded in 2017. The multipurpose venue became a concert hall for the Dresden Philharmonic Orchestra, and the detached structure on Wilsdruffer Strasse continues to provide a striking point of reference to the past.

14 Ingo Schulze, 'Ich war ein begeisterter Dresdner. Zum Auftakt der 800-Jahr Feier der sächsischen Hauptstadt – Nachtgedanken eines aus dem Ort Gefallenen', in *Süddeutsche Zeitung*, 31 March 2006.

Solitär in der Altstadt: der Kulturpalast zwischen Residenzschloss und Altmarkt. —— Distinctive structure in Dresden's historic centre: the Palace of Culture between the Royal Palace and Altmarkt square.

GROSSER HOF DES RESIDENZSCHLOSSES

Graffitis sind schnell hinterlassen, ein Sgraffito ist da schon etwas aufwendiger. Schließlich werden die ursprünglich aus Italien stammenden Verzierungen gekratzt statt gesprüht. Aus mehreren Lagen koloriertem Putz gehen so Flächenkunstwerke hervor. Die Dekorationen im großen Hof des Residenzschlosses entstanden im Zuge des Umbaus ab 1548 und wurden von deutschen Künstlern unter Anleitung der Italiener Francesco Ricchino sowie Gabriel und Benedetto Tola geschaffen. Wie Fritz Löffler ausführt, war es ausnahmsweise nicht der Krieg, der die detailverliebte Arbeit verschwinden ließ: „Sgraffitomalereien, die bald auch andere namhafte Gebäude der Stadt wie ein Teppich überzogen, gaben dem Dresden der Renaissance ein festliches Aussehen [...]. Leider waren in dem rauhen und feuchten Klima der Elbestadt alle malerischen Kunstwerke an den Außenwänden schon nach wenigen Jahrzehnten dem Untergang geweiht."[15] Bei der Wiedererrichtung des Schlosses entschied man sich auch für die Rückkehr der Fassade. Der federführende Baumeister sprach angesichts dessen vom „Achttausender unter den Schlössern"[16].

15 Fritz Löffler: *Das alte Dresden*, Leipzig 2012, S. 35 f.

16 Adina Rieckmann: „Ganz erbaulich". In: *Die Zeit*, Nr. 02/2012, 5.1.2012.

GREAT COURTYARD OF THE ROYAL PALACE

Whereas graffiti can be produced very quickly, the art of sgraffito, made by scratching rather than spraying, is a bit more time-consuming. In this decorative technique from Italy, works of art are etched into multiple layers of coloured plaster. The decorations in the great courtyard of the Royal Palace were created by German artists during the renovations begun in 1548, under the direction of the Italians Francesco Ricchino and Gabriel and Benedetto Tola. As Fritz Löffler explains, for once it was not the war that destroyed this intricate work: 'Sgraffito paintings soon also covered other well-known buildings in the city and gave Renaissance Dresden a festive appearance [...]. Unfortunately, all manner of artworks painted on exterior walls were doomed to fade after only a few decades given the raw, damp climate of the city on the Elbe.'[15] During the reconstruction of the palace, it was decided that this former facade would also be restored, prompting the lead architect to call this the 'Mount Everest of palaces'.[16]

15 Fritz Löffler, *Das alte Dresden* (Leipzig: 2012), pp. 35–36.

16 Adina Rieckmann, 'Ganz erbaulich', in *Die Zeit*, 5 January 2012.

1889

Zerkratzt und zerhauen: der große Hof des Residenzschlosses mit und ohne italienischer Dekoration. —— Scratched and battered: the great courtyard of the Royal Palace with and without Italian decoration.

nach 1945 —— after 1945

2013

STALLHOF DES RESIDENZSCHLOSSES

Wohin nur mit der Kutsche? Das fragte sich bereits Kurfürst Christian I. Der Stallhof wurde Ende des 16. Jahrhunderts errichtet. Obgleich einer der ältesten erhaltenen Turnierplätze der Welt, sind Pferde nur noch selten im Hof zu sehen. Dauerhaft allerdings findet man sie auf der Rückseite des sogenannten Langen Ganges, wo Zehntausende Fliesen aus Meißner Porzellan das Bild eines Reiterzuges entstehen lassen. Der Gang selbst verbindet die als Johanneum bezeichneten Stallungen mit dem Georgenbau, dem ersten Renaissancebauwerk der Stadt. Die Luftangriffe fügten dem Stallhof schwere Schäden zu, in einem Tagebucheintrag Victor Klemperers vom 30. April 1944 scheint sich die Katastrophe bereits anzukündigen: „Morgens Singen, Trommeln, Marschieren, Geschrei: Anmarsch und Aufstellung und Appell von Pimpfen, HJ- und BDM-Kolonnen auf der Carolabrücke. Irgendeine Feierlichkeit im Stallhof. Ich habe einen Abscheu vor dieser Entindividualisierung und Massenzurichtung. Aber offenbar ist sie Gesamtzeichen der Epoche."[17]

17 Victor Klemperer: *Ich will Zeugnis ablegen bis zum letzten: Tagebücher 1933–1945. Eine Auswahl*, Berlin 2012, S. 361.

STABLE COURTYARD OF THE ROYAL PALACE

Christian I, Elector of Saxony from 1586 to 1591, was already faced with the problem of where to keep his coach at the Royal Palace. The stable courtyard was then built at the end of sixteenth century. Despite being one of the oldest preserved tournament arenas in the world, horses are rarely seen in the courtyard today. However, they are a permanent feature of the so-called *Langer Gang* (Long Corridor), on the back of which the image of a procession of riders has been created using tens of thousands of Meissen porcelain tiles. The corridor itself connects the former royal stables, known as the Johanneum, and George's Gate, the city's first Renaissance structure. The stable courtyard was severely damaged by the aerial attacks of the Second World War. An entry in Victor Klemperer's diary on 30 April 1944 seems to foreshadow the impending catastrophe: 'In the morning singing, drumming, marching, shouts: assembly and line-up and roll-call of columns of Hitler Youth and League of German Girls on the Carola Bridge. Some ceremony in the Royal Mews. I abhor such de-individualisation and mass dressage. But evidently it is a mark of the epoch as a whole.'[17]

17 Victor Klemperer, *To the Bitter End. The Diaries of Victor Klemperer*, trans. by Martin Chalmers (London: 1999), p. 297.

Hü und hott: der Stallhof mit dem Kanz-
leihaus, dem Georgenbau und dem
„Langen Gang" (v. l. n. r.). —— Giddyup
and gee!—the stable courtyard with the
Chancellery, George's Gate, and the
'Long Corridor' (from left to right).

POSTPLATZ

„Den Postplatz hatte es übel zugerichtet", hielt der Dresdner Maler Otto Griebel in seinen Lebenserinnerungen, *Ich war ein Mann der Straße,* fest, „und es wirkte grotesk, wie inmitten dieses Chaos ausgerechnet die Rotunde der Dresdner Straßenbahn ohne besondere Beschädigungen stehengeblieben war."[18] Obschon heutzutage Mittelpunkt des städtischen Nahverkehrs, stockte am Postplatz die längste Zeit der Verkehr – noch bis ins 19. Jahrhundert verlief an dieser Stelle der Wassergraben der Festung Dresden. Aber bereits 1895 prägte das Schienenwirrwarr von sechs Tramtrassen das Einfallstor zur Wilsdruffer Vorstadt. Die Oberpostdirektion hatte da schon repräsentative Gebäude bezogen und war zum bestimmenden Element des Platzes geworden. Die Rotunde der Straßenbahn mag glimpflich davongekommen sein, schwere Schäden mussten allerdings u. a. vom Neuen Königlichen Schauspielhaus, vom Palasthotel Weber und von der Sophienkirche vermeldet werden. Letztere wurde 1962 unter großem Protest abgetragen. Bald nach der Wende wurde eine Umgestaltung des Areals anvisiert, die Arbeiten ziehen sich aber bis heute hin.

[18] Otto Griebel: *Ich war ein Mann der Straße. Lebenserinnerungen eines Dresdner Malers,* Leipzig 1986, S. 459.

POSTPLATZ

In his memoirs, *Ich war ein Mann der Strasse*, the Dresden painter Otto Griebel recalls, 'The Postplatz had been badly hit, and it was really quite grotesque how the rotunda of Dresden's tram system, of all things, had survived without any particular damage in the midst of this chaos.'[18] Although, today, the Postplatz is the centre of Dresden's urban transport, traffic stalled here for many years. The moat of Dresden's fortress had run past this site well into the nineteenth century, but by 1895, the junction to the Wilsdruffer suburbs was already a web of six tram lines. The Post Office Directorate had also moved into its representative building by this time and had become a defining element of the square. While the tram station's rotunda may have escaped serious damage, the New Royal Theatre, the Palasthotel Weber, and Saint Sophia's Church were not so lucky. The latter was removed in 1962 amid major protests. Plans to redesign the area were proposed soon after Germany's reunification, but construction has not been completed to this day.

[18] Otto Giebel, *Ich war ein Mann der Strasse. Lebenserinnerungen eines Dresdner Malers* (Leipzig: 1986), p. 459.

1928

1946

Seit jeher Verkehrsknotenpunkt der Stadt: der Postplatz. —— Postplatz: a hub of urban traffic from the start.

2007

KRONENTOR

39 Mio. Reichstaler, die Konversion zum Katholizismus und der Verlust wichtiger Ländereien – die Macht über Polen-Litauen lässt sich August der Starke einiges kosten. Um die Mitglieder der Ständeversammlung Sejm für sich zu gewinnen, veräußert er Besitztümer und zahlt reichlich Schmiergeld. Im 16. Jahrhundert hatte Sachsen noch den Schmalkaldischen Bund gegen die Katholische Liga angeführt, nun wendet sich der Kurfürst aus reinem Machtkalkül vom Protestantismus ab. 1697 besteigt er tatsächlich den Thron. ——— Zeugnis davon legt ein prachtvoller Pavillon des Zwingers ab. So tragen die vier Adler auf dem Giebel des Kronentores nicht etwa das Zeichen der Albertiner, sondern das Machtsymbol des polnischen Königs. Das von Matthäus Daniel Pöppelmann entworfene Portal hat den Krieg trotz großer Schäden überstanden und gilt heute als schönster Zugang des Komplexes. Sachsen-Polen war von deutlich kürzerer Dauer, bereits 1763 fiel die Krone an das Geschlecht der Poniatowskis. Und die sogenannte „Sachsenzeit" ist im Nachbarland als Episode maßloser Dekadenz in die Geschichte eingegangen.

CROWN GATE Thirty-nine million Reichstaler, the conversion to Catholicism, and the loss of important lands: Augustus the Strong was willing to pay a considerable price to rule the Polish-Lithuanian Commonwealth. In order to win over members of the Sejm, the parliament of the Kingdom of Poland, he sold properties and paid an abundance of bribes. In the sixteenth century, Saxony had led the Schmalkaldic League in the fight against the Catholic League. Now, however, the Elector had renounced Protestantism based solely on his desire for power, and, in 1697, he actually ascended the sought-after throne. ——— A magnificent pavilion at the Zwinger Palace bears witness to this event. Thus, the four eagles on the Crown Gate's summit display the Polish King's symbol of power rather than the sign of the Albertines. The gateway, designed by Matthäus Daniel Pöppelmann, survived the war despite extensive damage and, today, is considered the most beautiful entrance to the palace complex. The dominion of Saxony-Poland was short-lived. The crown fell to the Poniatowskis in 1763, and the so-called 'Saxony period' is remembered as an era of boundless decadence in the neighbouring state.

1900

1948

Augusteisches Zeitalter oder Sachsenzeit? Das Kronentor.
—— The Crown Gate: symbol of the Augustan era or the Saxony period?

2017

WALLPAVILLON

Auch wenn der Name noch die Nutzung als Verteidigungsanlage nahelegt, soll der Zwinger eher Festplatz denn Festung sein, als er Anfang des 18. Jahrhunderts errichtet wird. Auf Geheiß von August dem Starken legt Matthäus Daniel Pöppelmann eine Orangerie an, die in mehreren Etappen erweitert wird. Arbeiten des Bildhauers Balthasar Permoser tragen u. a. dazu bei, dass das Ensemble heute als Musterbeispiel des Barock gilt. ———— „Nach Stunden kamen wir an die Stelle, wo am Tag zuvor noch der Zwinger gestanden hatte", schrieb die Komponistin Aleida Montijn in *Nachrichten an K. G. Erinnerungen einer Komponistin* über die Zerstörung Dresdens. „Durch die rußige Dunstglocke konnte man kaum etwas sehen, die Augen waren inzwischen entzündet, aber der Zwinger war nicht mehr da. Anstelle dieses Kunstwerks war ein zehn Meter hoher Steinhaufen – aus dem erkennbare Teile des ehemaligen Zwingers ragten."[19] Eines der noch zu erahnenden Gebäude ist der Wallpavillon. Erst 1963 wird das architektonische Kunstwerk, das sich in der Bezeichnung als Wehranlage ausgibt, für die Öffentlichkeit wieder geöffnet.

[19] Aleida Montijn: *Nachrichten an K. G. Erinnerungen einer Komponistin*, Kassel 1988, S. 91.

WALL PAVILION

Even if the name still suggests its use as fortification, the Zwinger Palace (*Zwinger* referring to the outer ward of a castle) was intended as a place for court festivities rather than a fortress when it was built at the beginning of the eighteenth century. Originally an orangery built by the architect Matthäus Daniel Pöppelmann at the behest of Augustus the Strong, it was expanded in multiple stages. Due, among other things, to the works by the sculptor Balthasar Permoser, the architectural ensemble is considered the epitome of the Baroque. ———— In *Nachrichten an K.G. Erinnerungen einer Komponistin* (Messages for K.G. Memoirs of a Composer), the composer Aleida Montijn remembers the destruction of Dresden as follows: 'After several hours, we reached the spot where the Zwinger Palace had stood the day before. We could hardly see though the pall of soot and smoke, and our eyes were inflamed, but the Zwinger Palace was gone. In place of this work of art there stood a ten-metre high pile of rubble, from which recognisable parts of the former palace protruded.'[19] One of these familiar structures was the Wall Pavilion. The architectural work of art whose name evokes the image of a stronghold would be opened to the public once more, but not until 1963.

[19] Aleida Montijn, *Nachrichten an K. G. Erinnerungen einer Komponistin* (Kassel: 1988), p. 91.

Glanzstück barocker Baukunst: der Wallpavillon des Zwingers. —— A jewel of Baroque architecture: the Wall Pavilion at the
Zwinger Palace.

SEMPERGALERIE

Neben Canalettos berühmter Stadtansicht haben zwei weitere Gemälde der Galerie Alte Meister immer schon besondere Aufmerksamkeit erregt. „Wenn ich heute die Augen schließe und an die Schätze der Heimatstadt denke", resümiert beispielsweise Durs Grünbein im Aufsatz *Madonna und Venus*, „sehe ich ziemlich bald eine der beiden Frauen."[20] ——— Wenngleich bereits 1560 eine kurfürstliche Kunstkammer existierte, geht die Sammlung im Kern auf August den Starken und seinen Sohn Friedrich August II. zurück. Neben holländischen und flämischen Malern erwarben sie v. a. Gemälde der italienischen Renaissance. Ab 1855 wurden die Meisterwerke in einer Galerie am Zwinger gezeigt. ——— Während heute beim Besuch zumeist Raffaels *Sixtinische Madonna* in den Fokus rückt, stand für Grünbein seit jeher die *Schlummernde Venus*, das Hauptwerk des venezianischen Malers Giorgione, im Mittelpunkt: „Man will wissen, was hinter der Stirn vorgeht dieses schlafenden Menschen, erst recht wenn er nackt ist und eine Frau. Und schon ist man woanders und hat die Zeit vergessen. Solches geschieht hin und wieder in Dresden."[21]

[20] Durs Grünbein: „Madonna und Venus". In: Detlef Schöttker (Hg.): *Dresden: Eine literarische Einladung*, Berlin 2006, S. 87.

[21] Ebd., S. 97.

SEMPER GALLERY

Alongside Canaletto's famous view of the city, two other paintings in the Old Masters Gallery have always attracted particular attention. 'When I close my eyes today and think of the treasures in my home town', Durs Grünbein writes, for instance, in his essay *Madonna und Venus*, 'the image of one of these two women quickly comes to mind.'[20] ——— Although a royal art chamber already existed in 1560, the collection can, for the most part, be attributed to Augustus the Strong and his son Frederick Augustus II. In addition to works by Dutch and Flemish painters, they acquired several paintings from the Italian Renaissance, in particular. Beginning in 1855, the masterpieces were displayed in a gallery at the Zwinger Palace. ——— Whereas today's visitors are mainly drawn to Raphael's *Sistine Madonna*, Grünbein was always most fascinated by *The Sleeping Venus*, the principal work by the Venetian painter Giorgione: 'One wonders what thoughts are passing through the mind of this sleeping body, especially when the body is naked and that of a woman. And, suddenly, you forget where you are and lose track of the time. This happens now and then in Dresden.'[21]

[20] Durs Grünbein, 'Madonna und Venus', in *Eine literarische Einladung*, ed. by Detlef Schöttker (Berlin: 2006), p. 87.

[21] Ibid., p. 97.

1894

Hin und wieder in Dresden: die Semper-galerie. —— Now and then in Dresden: the Semper Gallery.

vor 1964 —— before 1964

2018

SEMPEROPER

Wagners *Tannhäuser* und *Der Fliegende Holländer*, *Der Rosenkavalier* sowie *Salome* von Richard Strauss – zahlreiche namhafte Werke erklangen erstmals in der Semperoper. Wie der Name schon deutlich macht, geht auch das Gebäude am Theaterplatz auf Entwürfe des Architekten Gottfried Semper zurück. ——— Zunächst war von 1838 bis 1841 das Königliche Hoftheater errichtet worden: „Das Theater ist gar nicht mehr schön zu nennen, sondern vollendet"[22], lobte seinerzeit Ida von Lüttichau, die Frau des damaligen Generalintendanten. Doch der Bau im Stil der italienischen Frührenaissance fiel bald einem Brand zum Opfer. ——— Obgleich er nach seiner Teilnahme am Maiaufstand aus der Stadt hatte fliehen müssen, legte Semper Pläne für den Neubau vor. 1878 wurde eine Oper fertiggestellt, auf deren Hauptportal bereits die markante Pantherquadriga Platz fand. Der Zweite Weltkrieg brachte erhebliche Schäden mit sich, doch wie heißt es in Carl Maria von Webers *Der Freischütz*, mit dem das rekonstruierte Haus 1985 wiedereröffnet worden war: „Und ob die Wolke sie verhülle, // Die Sonne bleibt am Himmelszelt."[23]

22 Petra Bern/Mondrian W. von Lüttichau (Hg.): *Wahrheit der Seele – Ida von Lüttichau (1798–1856). Ergänzungsband*, Berlin 2015, S. 67 f.

23 Carl Maria von Weber: *Der Freischütz. Oper in vier Abtheilungen*, Amsterdam 1825, S. 24.

SEMPER OPERA HOUSE

Richard Wagner's *Tannhäuser* and *The Flying Dutchman*, *The Knight of the Rose* and *Salome* by Richard Strauss: a number of celebrated works were first performed at the Semper Opera House. As indicated by the name, this building at Theaterplatz was also designed by the architect Gottfried Semper. ——— It was preceded by the Royal Court Theatre, which was built from 1838 to 1841 in the style of the early Italian Renaissance. 'The theatre cannot simply be called beautiful; it is perfection', Ida von Lüttichau, wife of the general director, extolled the building at the time.[22] However, the theatre was soon destroyed by a fire. ——— Despite the fact that Semper had been forced to flee the city after his participation in the May Uprising, he submitted plans for the new construction. The opera house was completed in 1878, at which time the main entrance already featured the distinctive Panther Quadriga. The Second World War resulted in considerable damage, but, to quote from Carl Maria von Weber's *The Marksman*, the first opera performed after the building was reconstructed in 1985, 'No matter if obscured by clouds, | The sun remains above us always.'[23]

22 *Wahrheit der Seele – Ida von Lüttichau (1798–1856). Ergänzungsband*, ed. by Petra Bern and Mondrian W. von Lüttichau (Berlin: 2015), pp. 67–68.

23 Carl Maria von Weber, *Der Freischütz. Oper in vier Abtheilungen* (Amsterdam: 1825), p. 24.

Vollendung und Zerstörung: die Semperoper. —— Perfection and destruction: the
Semper Opera House.

DRESDEN VOM ELBUFER

Zahlreiche Schätze hat die Kunstsammlung Alte Meister zu bieten, doch kaum ein Gemälde hat die Wahrnehmung Dresdens derart beeinflusst wie eine Vedute von Bernardo Bellotto, genannt Canaletto: „Ansicht von Dresden. Vom rechten Elbufer unterhalb der Augustusbrücke. Die Elbe fliesst vom Hintergrunde links zum Vordergrunde rechts herab. Rechts, am jenseitigen Ufer, die katholische Hofkirche, die Brücke, die Kuppel der Frauenkirche. Vorn links ein Haus neben einem Baume. Davor am Ufer verschiedene Staffage-Figuren."[24] Die nüchterne Beschreibung im Katalog der Königlichen Gemäldegalerie aus dem Jahr 1887 liefert kaum Hinweise darauf, dass noch heute vom „Canaletto-Blick" die Rede ist, wenn sich Elbe, Augustusbrücke und Schloss in entsprechender Konstellation befinden. Bellotto, der das ursprüngliche Werk 1748 als Hofmaler von Friedrich August II. schuf, fertigte von der Stadtansicht weitere Fassungen an. Eine schmückte einst das Büro Erich Honeckers und hängt heute im Amtszimmer des Bundespräsidenten im Schloss Bellevue.

[24] Karl Woermann: „Die italienischen Schulen. III. Die Italiener bis zum Ende des XVII. und XVIII. Jahrhunderts". In: Generaldirection der Königlichen Sammlungen für Kunst und Wissenschaft (Hg.): *Katalog der Königlichen Gemäldegalerie zu Dresden*, Dresden 1887, S. 205.

DRESDEN AS SEEN FROM THE ELBE RIVERBANK
The Old Masters Gallery includes a number of treasures, but a veduta by Bernardo Bellotto, known as Canaletto, has influenced the idea of Dresden like no other painting: 'Dresden from the Right Bank of the Elbe below the Augustus Bridge. The Elbe River flows from left to right, from the background to the foreground. To the right, on the opposite river bank, the court's Catholic church, the bridge, the dome of the Church of Our Lady. To the left, in the foreground, a house next to a tree. In front of these, a variety of staffage.'[24] Based on this sober description in the catalogue of the Royal Gallery of Paintings from the year 1887, one would hardly guess that, even today, a particular constellation of Elbe, Augustus Bridge, and palace is still described as a 'Canaletto view'. Bellotto, the court painter who created the original artwork for Frederick Augustus II in 1748, also painted other versions of this cityscape. One of these once decorated Erich Honecker's office and, today, hangs in that of the Federal President at Bellevue Palace.

[24] Karl Woermann, 'Die italienischen Schulen. III. Die Italiener bis zum Ende des XVII. und XVIII. Jahrhunderts', in *Katalog der Königlichen Gemäldegalerie zu Dresden*, ed. by Generaldirection der Königlichen Sammlungen für Kunst und Wissenschaft (Dresden: 1887), p. 205.

Sächsisches Ständehaus, Residenzschloss und Katholische Hofkirche (v.l.n.r.) – im Gegensatz zum berühmten Canaletto-Gemälde allerdings vom Elbufer oberhalb der Augustusbrücke betrachtet. —— The Parliamentary Building of Saxony, the Royal Palace, and the Catholic Court Church (from left to right)—in contrast to the famous Canaletto painting, however, the view is from the Elbe riverbank above the Augustus Bridge.

DER GOLDENE REITER

Kräftig soll August der Starke gewesen sein, derart urgewaltig, dass er ein Hufeisen mit bloßen Händen verbogen haben soll. Doch dies allein mag nicht Ausschlag gegeben haben, ihn auf einem Lipizzanerhengst reitend darzustellen. Vielmehr zeigt die Statue einen Regenten vom Format römischer Befehlshaber, überlebensgroß, energisch und den Blick streng gen Polen gerichtet, über das August ab 1697 gleichwohl herrschte. Der Goldene Reiter wurde 1736, drei Jahre nach dem Tod des sächsischen Kurfürsten, auf dem Neustädter Markt platziert und schwang sich zum Wahrzeichen der Stadt auf, das u.a. auf dem Qualitätssiegel der Dresdner Christstollen zu sehen ist. ——— Auch um das Standbild selbst ranken sich Legenden. So soll Ludwig Wiedemann, der ausführende Kupferschmied, der kunstvollen Aufgabe nur unter Zuhilfenahme des Teufels gewachsen gewesen sein. Doch als der diabolische Beistand ihn verließ, bevor er dem Tier eine Zunge ins Maul setzen konnte, gingen Wiedemann die Pferde durch und er starb auf der Stelle.

THE GOLDEN HORSEMAN
Augustus the Strong is said to have been a physically powerful man, so powerful, in fact, that he supposedly bent a horseshoe with his bare hands. Yet this may not have been the decisive reason for portraying him as a rider on a Lipizzaner stallion. Rather, the statue depicts a sovereign with the stature of a Roman general—larger than life, energetic, and gazing sternly in the direction of Poland, over which Augustus also ruled as of 1697. The Golden Rider was erected at Neustädter Markt in 1736, three years after the Elector of Saxony's death, and ascended to become a symbol of the city, as seen, for instance, in the seal of quality found on Dresdner Christstollen, the famous Christmas cake from the region. ——— Various legends have also sprung up around the statue itself. For instance, Ludwig Wiedemann, the executing coppersmith, was said to have required the devil's assistance in completing his artistically demanding task. But when his diabolical helper abandoned him before he was able to finish the horse's tongue, Wiedemann went into a frenzy and died on the spot.

1885

1945

Ritt durch die Zeiten: der Neustädter Markt mit dem Denkmal für, so die Übersetzung der Inschrift, „Friedrich August I. // Herzog von Sachsen, Kurfürst und Erzmarschall des Heiligen Römischen Reiches, König von Polen. // August II." —— A ride through the ages: Neustädter Markt with the monument to 'Frederick Augustus I | Duke of Saxony, Elector and Highest Marshal of the Holy Roman Empire, King of Poland. | Augustus II', as the translation of the inscription reads.

2013

CAROLABRÜCKE

„Dresden hat eine große, feierliche Lage", schrieb Heinrich von Kleist 1801 in einem Brief an seine Verlobte, Wilhelmine von Zenge, „in der Mitte der umkränzenden Elbhöhen, die in einiger Entfernung, als ob sie aus Ehrfurcht nicht näher zu treten wagten, es umlagern. Der Strom [...] schlängelt sich spielend in tausend Umwegen durch das freundliche Tal, als wollte er nicht in das Meer."[25] ——— Vier Brücken führen im Innenstadtbereich über die Elbe, die ursprüngliche Carolabrücke wurde 1895 eröffnet. Ihr Name geht auf die Ehefrau von Albert I. und letzte Königin von Sachsen, Carola von Wasa-Holstein-Gottorp, zurück. Bevor die Rote Armee die Brücke erreichen konnte, wurde sie am 7. Mai 1945, das heißt einen Tag vor dem Ende des Zweiten Weltkrieges in Europa, von den Deutschen gesprengt. ——— Überdauert haben Nereide und Triton, zwei Figuren die sinnbildlich für die „ruhige" bzw. „bewegte Elbe" stehen und am südlichen Brückenkopf zu finden sind. Der Folgebau wurde 1971 fertiggestellt, er ist heute der am stärksten frequentierte innerstädtische Übergang über den Fluss, der sich noch 664 Kilometer „Zeit lässt", bis er bei Hamburg ins Meer mündet.

[25] Heinrich von Kleist: *Briefe Heinrich von Kleists*, Leipzig 1925, S. 143.

CAROLA BRIDGE

'Dresden is situated in a large and festive space', Heinrich von Kleist wrote in a letter to his fiancée, Wilhelmine von Zenge, in 1801, 'in the midst of the hilltops encircling the Elbe Valley from some distance, as if too much in awe to draw nearer. The river [...] playfully winds through the friendly valley in a roundabout way, as if reluctant to enter the sea.'[25] ——— Four bridges lead across the Elbe River in the city centre. The original Carola Bridge, opened in 1895, was named for the wife of Albert I and last Queen of Saxony, Carola von Wasa-Holstein-Gottorp. On 7 May 1945, one day before the end of the Second World War in Europe, the bridge was demolished by German forces before the Red Army could reach it. ——— The bridge's destruction was survived by the figures of Nereid and Triton, the symbols of a 'calm' and 'tubulent Elbe' located at the southern bridgehead. The new construction was completed in 1971 and is the most heavily frequented inner-city bridge across the river, which 'takes its time' for another 664 kilometres before running into the sea near Hamburg.

[25] Heinrich von Kleist, *Briefe Heinrich von Kleists* (Leipzig: 1925), p. 143.

1928

1952

Mit Nereide und Triton: die Carolabrücke in bewegten und ruhigen Zeiten. —— Nereid and Triton: the Carola Bridge in calm and turbulent times.

2018

STRASSBURGER PLATZ

Mit etwas Geduld sieht man sie vielleicht, die sogenannte Car-GoTram, eine Güterstraßenbahn der Dresdner Verkehrsbetriebe, die Bauteile vom VW-Logistik-Zentrum im Stadtteil Friedrichstadt zum Straßburger Platz transportiert. Auch wenn die moderne Architektur in diesem Fall kaum Hinweise liefert, steht die Gläserne Manufaktur des Autobauers nichtsdestotrotz in der Tradition der ehemaligen Bebauung am nördlichen Ende des Großen Gartens. ——— Denn von 1896 bis zum Zweiten Weltkrieg hatte sich an dieser Stelle der Städtische Ausstellungspalast befunden. Das im Stil der Neorenaissance gehaltene Hauptgebäude wurde von einem Verwaltungstrakt sowie einem Musikpavillon ergänzt. Die Anlage, mit der Zeit immer weiter ausgebaut, bot zahlreichen bedeutenden Werkschauen Platz, etwa in den Bereichen Gartenbau, Kunst und Hygiene. Zu DDR-Zeiten wurden mit einem Ausstellungszentrum wiederum Präsentationsflächen geschaffen. Zur Eröffnung 1969 waren bereits die ersten Hochhäuser in Plattenbauweise entstanden, die den zwischenzeitlich zum Verkehrsknotenpunkt gewachsenen Platz bis heute prägen.

STRASSBURGER PLATZ With a bit of patience, visitors to Dresden might spot the so-called CarGoTram, a freight tram operated by Dresdner Verkehrsbetriebe that transports supplies to Strassburger Platz from the Volkswagen logistics centre in the district of Friedrichstadt. Despite its modern architecture, the car manufacturer's transparent factory building actually follows the tradition of former construction at the northern end of the Grand Garden. ——— From 1896 until the Second World War, this site was home to the city's Exhibition Palace. The neo-Renaissance-style main building was supplemented by an administrative wing and a music pavilion, and the complex was continually expanded over time. It housed several notable exhibitions, including on topics relating to horticulture, art, and hygiene. During the GDR era, a new exhibition centre was built to provide an area for presentations. By the time of its inauguration in 1969, the first concrete-slab high-rises had already been erected here, and the square, which has transformed into a hub of traffic today, is still characterised by these prefabricated structures.

Vergangene wie aktuelle Präsentationsflächen am Straßburger Platz. An Stelle des zerstörten Stübelbrunnens wurde 1963 ein Denkmal für den tschechischen Schriftsteller Julius Fučík eingeweiht. —— Former and current presentation areas at Strassburger Platz. A monument to the Czech writer Julius Fučik was erected in place of the destroyed Stübel Fountain in 1963.

PALAIS
IM GROSSEN GARTEN

Als wären die Elbauen nicht genug, weiß Dresden auch noch mit einem Park im Geiste französischer Gartenarchitektur aufzuwarten. Den Anstoß gab Johann Georg III. (1647–1691), der sich einen kurfürstlichen Jagdgarten vor den Festungswerken wünschte. Im Zentrum des Großen Gartens befindet sich ein frühbarockes Palais, das von Kavalierhäusern umgeben ist. Das Lustschloss wurde im Zweiten Weltkrieg schwer getroffen und ist bis dato nicht vollends wiederhergestellt. Der Zoo, seit 1861 Bestandteil des Parks, beklagte den Verlust fast aller Tiere. In Marcel Beyers Roman *Kaltenburg* hat eine Horde Affen überlebt, die sich – einem offenbar traumatisierten Überlebenden zufolge – nach den Luftangriffen gar sonderbar verhalten haben soll: „Mit gesenktem Blick forschen die Überlebenden nach bekannten Gesichtern. Irgendwann beginnen auch die Schimpansen, die Züge der reglos am Boden liegenden Gestalten zu betrachten, man könnte glauben, sie sähen abwechselnd den Toten und den Lebenden ratsuchend in die Augen."[26]

26 Marcel Beyer: *Kaltenburg*, Frankfurt a. M. 2009, S. 16 f.

THE GRAND GARDEN PALACE
As if the meadows along the Elbe River were not enough, Dresden also boasts a park in the spirit of French garden design. The project was initiated by Johann Georg III (1647-1691), who wanted a royal hunting ground in front of the fortifications. At the centre of the Grand Garden sits an early-Baroque palace surrounded by smaller houses for visiting nobility. The pleasure palace was badly damaged during the Second World War and, to this day, has not been completely restored. The zoo, which has been part of the park since 1861, suffered the loss of almost all its animals. In Marcel Beyer's novel *Kaltenburg*, a horde of monkeys survives and, according to an apparently traumatised witness, begins to behave in a rather peculiar manner after the air strikes: 'Eyes on the ground, the survivors search for familiar faces. At some point the chimpanzees too begin to scrutinize the features of the motionless figures; you might almost imagine they are looking for guidance from the eyes of the living and the dead in turn.'[26]

26 Marcel Beyer, *Kaltenburg*, trans. by Alan Bance (New York: 2012), p. 10.

1890

Auftakt des „Dresdner Barocks": das Palais im Großen Garten. —— The beginning of 'Dresden Baroque': the Grand Garden Palace.

1946

2013

YENIDZE

Der Bau einer Moschee sorgt in Dresden für Aufruhr. Doch befinden wir uns nicht etwa in der Gegenwart, wie man vorschnell annehmen könnte – die Yenidze gibt es bereits seit 1909. Hugo Zietz hatte damals eine Zigarettenfabrik errichten wollen, doch war es zu jener Zeit verboten, Industrieanlagen in die Innenstadt zu setzen. Die Idee, der Fabrik das Antlitz einer Moschee zu verleihen, kam ihm auf einer Orientreise. Der beauftragte Architekt, Martin Hammitzsch, soll sich am Grabmal des Emirs Khair Bak in Kairo orientiert haben, den Schornstein verbarg er in einem Minarett. Der Name der Orientalischen Tabak- und Zigarettenfabrik „Yenidze" leitete sich von einem osmanischen Anbaugebiet ab, aus dem das Unternehmen größtenteils seinen Tabak bezog. Das markante Gebäude wurde von vermeintlichen Bewahrern des Dresdner Barocks angegriffen, Hammitzsch gar aus der Reichsarchitektenkammer ausgeschlossen. Allerdings erwies sich die exotisierende Aufmachung als überaus werbewirksam und ließ Zietz zu einem Schwergewicht der Branche aufsteigen, ehe er 1924 an Reemtsma verkaufte. Heute rauchen in der Yenidze nur noch die Köpfe, sind doch Büros in ihr untergebracht.

YENIDZE The construction of a mosque caused a considerable uproar in Dresden—but not in this day and age, as one might assume. The Yenidze building exists since 1909. At the time, Hugo Zietz had wanted to build a cigarette factory; however, in those days, industrial facilities were not permitted in the city centre. The idea to give the factory the appearance of a mosque came to Zietz while travelling through the Middle East. The commissioned architect, Martin Hammitzsch, is said to have based his design on the Amir Khayrbak Funerary Complex in Cairo. The smokestack was hidden in a minaret. 'Yenidze', the name of the Middle-Eastern-style tobacco and cigarette factory, derives from the Ottoman region where the company obtained most of its tobacco. The distinctive building was attacked by supposed guardians of Dresden's Baroque, and Hammitzsch was even excluded from the Reich Chamber of Architects. Nevertheless, the exotic construction proved to be a thoroughly effective advertising tool and helped Zietz to become a prominent figure in the tobacco industry before he sold the factory to Reemtsma in 1924. Today, the only cigarettes at Yenidze would be those belonging to the workers in what is now an office building.

Pfiffig und provokativ: die „Tabakmoschee" Yenidze.
—— Ingenious and provocative: the 'tobacco mosque' Yenidze.

Bildnachweis —— Photo credits

akg-images: S. 71 o., 15; akg-images/André Held: S. 9; akg-images/arkivi: S. 25 o.; akg-images/Bildarchiv Monheim: S. 61 u.; akg-images/Bildarchiv Pisarek: S. 14; akg-images/picture alliance/ZB: S. 35 o. l.; akg-images/picture-alliance/ZB/Ulrich Hässler: S. 51 u.; akg-images/Sammlung Berliner Verlag/Archiv: S. 13, 33 o.; Barbara Schlesinger: nach S. 53; Dresden-Karten: „Data CC BY-SA by OpenStreetMap"; © 4UMaps.com ; © OpenStreetMap and contributors, CC BY-SA; Götz Walter/verschwundene-bauwerke.de: S. 27 u.; SLUB Dresden/Deutsche Fotothek: S. 23 M. (Walter Hahn), 27 M. (unbek.), 29 o. (Verlag A. und R. Adam), 29 M. (Alfred Wernicke), 31 o. (Max Nowak), 31 M. (Walter Hahn), 33 M. (Walter Hahn), 35 M. (Ermenegildo Antonio Donadini), 35 o. (Richard Peter sen.), 37 u. und Cover o. (Richard Peter jun.), 39 M. (Paul Schulz), 39 o. l. (Walter Möbius), 41 o. (Alfred Wernicke), 41 M. (Alfred Wernicke), 43 l. (Walter Möbius), 43 u. (Walter Möbius), 45 o. (Walter Möbius), 45 M. (Gerhard Döring), 47 o. (Ermenegildo Antonio Donadini), 47 u. (unbek.), 49 o. (Heinz Märker), 49 M. (Richard Peter sen.), 51 o. (Trinks und Co. GmbH Leipzig), 51 M. (Richard Peter sen.), 53 li. (Ermenegildo Antonio Donadini), 55 o. r. (Walter Hahn), 55 M. (Alfred Wernicke), 57 o. (Hermann Krone), 57 M. (Richard Peter sen.), 59 o. (Walter Möbius), 59 M. (Walter Hahn), 61 o. (Arno Jahr), 61 M. (Walter Möbius), 63 o. (Hermann Krone), 65 o. (unbek.), 65 M. (unbek.), 67 o. (Landesverein Sächs. Heimatschutz), 67 M. (Paul Schulz), 67 u. (Inger Sørensen), 69 o. (Hermann Krone), 69 M. (Walter Möbius); Mauritius images: S. 19 (Günter Gräfenhain), 31 u. (Gunter Kirsch/alamy), 33 u. (imageBROKER/Frank Bienewald), 39 u. (Westend61/Torsten Becker), 43 u. (imageBROKER/Michael Nitzschke), 59 u. (imageBROKER/Gabriele Hanke), 71 u. (Frank Bienewald/Alamy); tilialucida/Alamy Stock Photo: Cover u. r.,S. 37 u.; alle übrigen Abb. —— all other images: Wikimedia Commons

Impressum —— Imprint

Bibliografische Information der Deutschen Nationalbibliothek

Die Deutsche Nationalbibliothek verzeichnet diese Publikation in der Deutschen Nationalbibliografie; detaillierte bibliografische Daten sind im Internet über http://dnb.dnb.de abrufbar. —— German National Library bibliographical information: The German National Library lists this publication in the German National Bibliography; detailed bibliographical information is available online at http://dnb.dnb.de.

Karl-Tauchnitz-Str. 6 | D–04107 Leipzig

produktsicherheit@seemann-henschel.de | www.seemann-henschel.de | instagram.com/seemann_henschel_verlagsgruppe | facebook.com/seemann.henschel | pinterest.de/seemann_henschel

ISBN 978-3-86502-421-3

Umschlaggestaltung —— Cover design: flamboyant books, Maria Rajka
Gestaltung und Satz —— Layout und typesetting: Gudrun Hommers, Berlin
Projektmanagement —— Project management: Caroline Keller, Iris Klein, Thea Ferber
Lektorat —— Editing: Iris Klein
Übersetzung —— Translation: Kristine Jennings, Berlin
Korrektorat Englisch —— Proofreading English: Uli Nickel, Münster
Herstellung —— Production: Arnold & Domnick, Leipzig
Lithografie —— Lithography: Bild1Druck, Berlin
Druck und Bindung —— Printing and binding: bittner print s.r.o., Bratislava

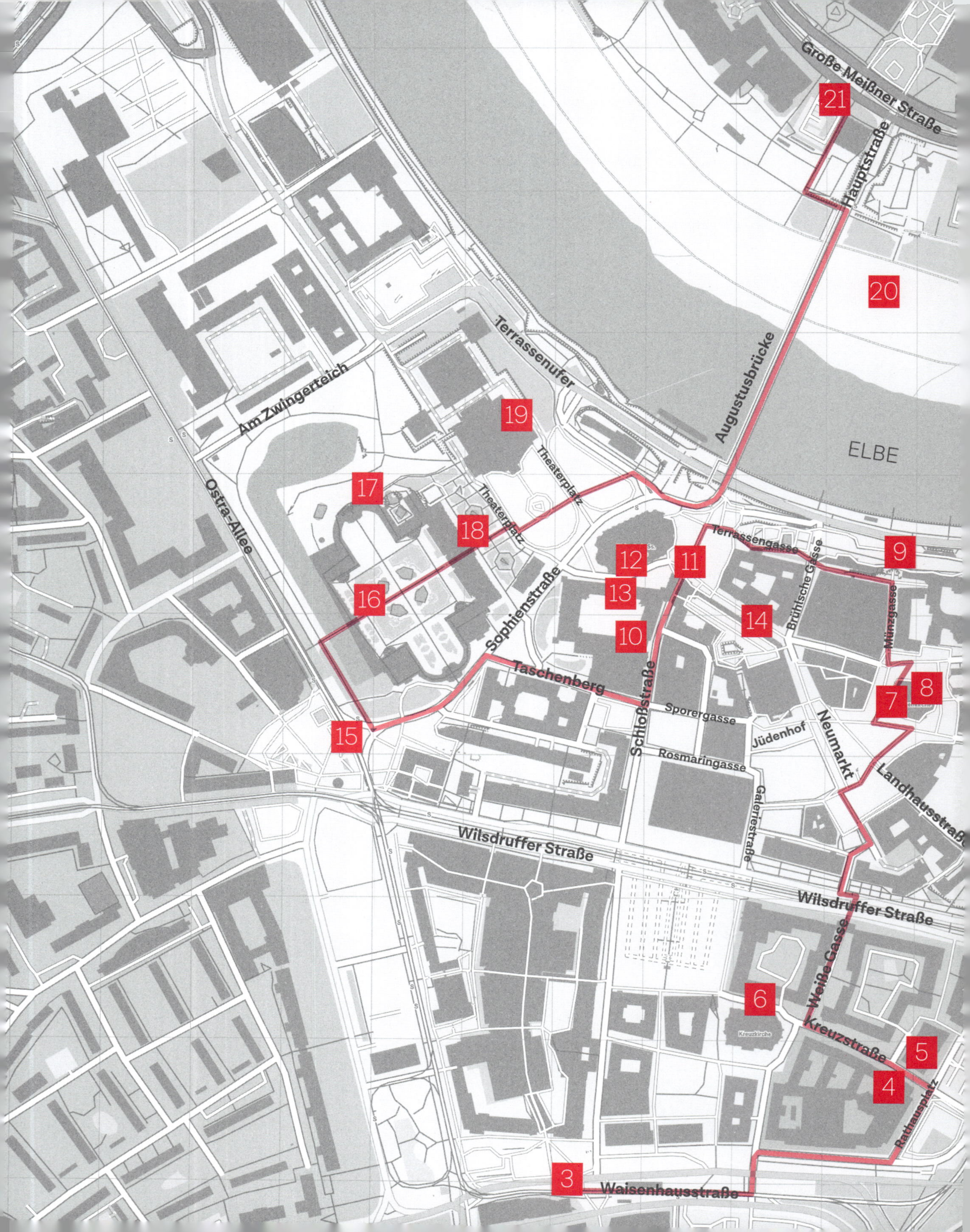

Große Meißner Straße
21
Hauptstraße
20
Terrassenufer
Augustusbrücke
ELBE
Am Zwingerteich
19
Theaterplatz
17
Theaterplatz
18
9
Ostra-Allee
Terrassengasse
16
12
11
Brühlsche Gasse
13
14
Münzgasse
Sophienstraße
10
8
Taschenberg
Schloßstraße
7
Sporergasse
Jüdenhof
Neumarkt
15
Rosmaringasse
Landhausstraße
Galeriestraße
Wilsdruffer Straße
Wilsdruffer Straße
6
Weiße Gasse
Kreuzkirche
Kreuzstraße
5
4
3
Waisenhausstraße
Rathausplatz